Becoming a New Creation in Christ

A BIBLICAL GUIDE ON HOW TO GET THE MOST OUT OF YOUR LIFE AND RELATIONSHIPS

Russell Frahm

TRILOGY CHRISTIAN PUBLISHERS

TUSTIN, CA

Trilogy Christian Publishers

A Wholly Owned Subsidary of Trinity Broadcasting Network

2442 Michelle Drive

Tustin, CA 92780

For information, address Trilogy Christian Publishing

Rights Department, 2442 Michelle Drive, Tustin, Ca 92780.

Trilogy Christian Publishing/ TBN and colophon are trademarks of Trinity Broadcasting Network.

For information about special discounts for bulk purchases, please contact Trilogy Christian Publishing.

Manufactured in the United States of America

Trilogy Disclaimer: The views and content expressed in this book are those of the author and may not necessarily reflect the views and doctrine of Trilogy Christian Publishing or the Trinity Broadcasting Network.

10 9 8 7 6 5 4 3 2 1

Library of Congress Cataloging-in-Publication Data is available.

ISBN 978-1-63769-400-8

ISBN 978-1-63769-401-5 (ebook)

Contents

Dedication

I dedicate this book to my mother, Joan Frahm. She worked for many years as a head nurse in oncology in our community hospital. She was a very sensitive person, cared about her patients, and cared about me. In a sense, I was one of her patients because I needed someone like her to make it through adolescence! I always knew she was there for me and loved me even when I was not behaving in a healthy way. I was not a good student in high school. I never brought a book home. Never! Spending time with girls and making money was more important to me at that time than books or studies. With that being said, I ended up in the top twenty percent in my High School class of about six hundred students. My mother would often ask during those years, "Don't you have homework?" I would tell her I had already finished it. She would smile and shake her head. My mom taught me about grace. She taught me about undeserved favor. I knew no matter what I did or did not do, she loved me and accepted me. That is powerful. It is the way God is with us. My mother is now with the Lord in heaven. She died suddenly in 1996 at the age of sixty-five. I still miss her to this day. I will always miss her. She taught me a lot about how to know you are loved unconditionally. She taught me a lot about love, the kind of love that God has for us. That is what I want to write about in this book: how to love like God loves us.

I also dedicate this book to my wife, Karen. We raised four children together, have been married for over forty years, and partners in ministry for thirty-eight years. She has been a tireless worker in the church and a great support for me. I often have said to my people in the church, "My wife is the best pastor's wife anyone could have." She challenges me. She believes in me. She supports me. She keeps me in line. God has used her as His chosen instrument to shape and mold me in Christ. Sometimes that hurts. Sometimes that process has been a wonderful nurturing experience. I could not have accomplished the things I have done in ministry without her love and support. For that, I am grateful!

I also dedicate this book to the great many people who have met with me in the counseling office. I will share some of their stories in this book, but of course, protect their identity. After thousands of counseling appointments, I have heard just about everything human beings can go through in life. I have learned a great deal from people in the counseling office, and I want to thank them for trusting me.

Finally, I want to dedicate this book to Ida Mall, a lady who laughed when I told her some thirty-two years ago that I wanted to write a book. She did not believe that I could write a book...at least not a book that anyone would want to read. I do not write this book to prove anything to Ida. I am writing this book because I want to share my heart. After all, would not that be my unique contribution to the world? May God use the material in this book in any way that He chooses.

Let's go on a journey together. A journey of the heart. A journey with the Spirit of God. A journey to become in ever-increasing measure a new creation in Christ.

Acknowledgements

First, I am thankful for my wife, Karen, who supported me in the writing of this book. She read and reread the manuscript several times, making many helpful comments. She also verified that the material in this book is true!

I am also thankful to Janice Cheshire, a Brevard County School Educator, who edited the manuscript for grammar corrections and gave many helpful suggestions.

I am also thankful to my four children, Matthew, Philip, Stephen, and Judith, who allowed me to share stories from their lives.

I am also thankful to the people of Faith Lutheran Church, Merritt Island, Florida, for supporting me as their pastor for thirty-two years and for sharing their life experiences with me.

Foreword

"Russell has given us a gift. The promise of 2 Corinthians 5:17: 'Therefore, if anyone is in Christ, he is a new creation...' is the basis for this skillfully written work of art! Dr. Frahm takes us into virtually every aspect of our lives and challenges us to live in the promise God has given, that we are New Creations in Christ.

"Pastor Frahm's words have encouraged me. His writing is uncommonly clear, engaging and reveals a man of compassion and total honesty. This book will encourage you for your New Life in Christ!

"I couldn't put it down! Thanks, Russell."

Rev. Thomas Zehnder
Former President of the Florida-Georgia District of the
Lutheran Church-Missouri Synod.
Also served as executive director of LCMS World Missions.

"It is not often that a book speaks so clearly, that you can immediately see what needs to change in your life. Pragmatic, honest, and scripturally 'on point,' Dr. Frahm journeys with his readers through common life experiences to pose questions we must all ask ourselves as New Creations in Christ. As I initially edited this book as a friend *of Russ and the Frahm family (having even taught his children), I couldn't put it down! Truly, Dr. Frahm's writing is inspired by the Holy Spirit with its straightforward approach to living well. While there are no shortcuts in our spiritual journey, this book is the Cliffs-Notes you put in your back pocket as a trusted guide."*

Janice Cheshire
National Board Certified Teacher

Preface

I have been a pastor for thirty-eight years. I have dealt with a lot of people in the good and the bad of life. I have an advanced degree in counseling, and for a period of five years, I was the head of a counseling ministry with two licensed counselors meeting with people from the community at our church. The reason I started a counseling center at the church was that I was having so many people contact me for counseling that I could no longer handle the requests. I was scheduling twenty or more counseling appointments a month as well as being the pastor of a church. As a pastor, besides meetings, worship services, weddings, funerals, and other administrative duties, I have had countless hours of counseling with people. I want to share my experiences in counseling and as a pastor. I want to share my heart. I have thought about writing a book for a long time, but church and family commitments always seemed more important. Having just retired from full-time ministry, I felt a need, no, a calling to write. I hope the material in this book is beneficial to you and helps you become a new creation in Christ!

It is my philosophy of life that the heart is what matters. I have seen enough people putting on an act, doing what is expected, playing the game, and/or just "going through the motions" without considering the heart of the matter. I can't do that. I won't do that. If what I am doing does not speak to my heart, to your heart, to anyone's heart, then why do it? So, at times I am emotionally blunt, raw, real, candid (sorry, family!). I want to speak from my heart to your heart. I can do no other.

Living on the surface is so much safer, superficial, serene. To go deeper is risky, exciting, fulfilling. I invite you to go on a journey with me. The journey is to explore the depth of the heart of God and our own hearts. That is what I did and what I asked people to do whenever I gave a sermon. I asked people to go on a journey with me. Sometimes that journey was very emotional. Sometimes it meant laughter, sometimes tears, sometimes anger. But it was a journey. Do you have your bags packed for the journey toward becoming a new creation in Christ? You don't need suitcases for this journey, only your heart and your faith in God. No one can fully explore the depths of God's heart. That is a lifetime journey.

Let's explore some of the hearts of God together in this book. And let's try to change our hearts to be more like the heart of God. Becoming like Christ is a lifelong journey. It is what we call in theology, sanctification. I will write more about the theology of becoming a new creation in Christ later in this book. The elements of the life-long journey of becoming new creations in Christ are what I want to address in this book. I hope you will evaluate each area of your life as to how you are becoming a new creation in Christ. As I have said to people numerous times in the counseling situation, "nothing changes until something changes." When it comes to being a new creation in Christ, nothing changes until something changes. Thankfully, God, by His Holy Spirit, is a change agent. God loves us enough to save us from sin and death. God also loves us enough so that He wants us to grow in His love and truth. God wants us to be on the journey of becoming new creations in Christ.

Introduction

This book deals with twelve areas of our life. This book is a guide to help the reader evaluate each of these twelve areas to evaluate how well they are becoming a new creation in Christ. At the end of each chapter, there are questions to help the reader evaluate how they are doing with the material in this book. The book can be used for personal growth, for growth in marriage, for premarital couples, and for discussion in a small group. It is my hope that the material in this book will lead to a change in the life of the reader. It is my hope that, with these changes, people will become more like Christ.

Recently my wife and I were on a trip to Silver Creek, Mississippi. Total heartbeat of the world! We were visiting my sister and brother-in-law. They had retired some months before our trip and bought a "farm" house in Silver Creek, a town of 200 people. We had just retired from thirty-eight years of ministry. I had retired as a full-time pastor and my wife, Karen, as Music Director in the church. As I walked through my sister's kitchen, I stopped short and just stared. That's an interesting decoration, I thought to myself. It was a growth chart. You know, the kind of chart where you mark the growth of your children through time. The interesting thing is that my sister's children are all grown. My sister and brother-in-law no longer live in the house where their children grew up. It was a wood growth chart. The growth chart we used when our children grew up was of paper and had long since been thrown away. Some people mark their children's growth chart on a wall, and when the children grow up, they paint that wall and the growth chart. So, why would someone keep a growth chart? And why would they put it up in the corner of their kitchen? Simple. It was a symbol of the past. It gave a visual reminder of where their family had been in one chapter of their lives. It helped them to remember that their children were young at one time but that they had grown past that stage. It reminded them of a time in the past. The growth chart was a visual representation of where they had been. There were marks where each child reached a particular milestone of growth and the date when they reached that milestone.

Here is the point. If you had a Christian life growth chart, what milestones would be noted there? What stages have you gone through? It is clear in the Scriptures that God wants us to be like Christ. To be mature. To reach the full measure of the stature of Christ. What does that look like to grow into the full measure of the stature of Christ? That is the subject of this book. To be Christ-like. Becoming like Christ is a lifelong process. We never will grow out of that process until we die and go to heaven. We never will arrive at the position of being fully like Christ in this world. But God is faithful to move us along in this process and to ultimately complete the process. The process will be completed when we finally enter heaven by faith in Christ, who is the resurrection and the life. When we enter heaven, we will see Christ face to face. In heaven, we will take hold of that for which Christ Jesus took hold of us. We will be transformed. But in this life, we are still a work in progress. The question is, are we moving along in the process, are we stuck in the process, or are we moving away from the goal, which is becoming new creations in Christ? I hope you will say with me that you want to be, in ever-increasing measure, more like Christ. You want to be moving along in the process of becoming more like Christ.

It has been said that you can't teach an old dog new tricks. What is implied by this statement is that people reach a point in their life when they cannot, or will not, change. That cannot be the norm for people who have been redeemed by Christ. We are to keep growing. We want to become the person for which Christ redeemed us. We are all, as believers in Christ, in a life-long process of growing into the likeness of Christ. We are all, no matter what age, becoming new creations in Christ.

So, where are you at in your relationship with Christ? Are you evidencing the fruit of the Spirit (Galatians 5) in ever-increasing quality in all aspects of your life? Can you say that, in the last year of your life, you are more loving, more joyful, more at peace? Can you truly say, "I am not what I used to be, and I am not what I am going to be?" When people are around you, do they say, or at least think, "I see Christ in you?" What experiences, what truths, what changes would you note on your spiritual growth chart? Even more than that, would you be bold enough to publish them for everyone to see? That would be your testimony. Your testimony is not only about how God called you from sin and death to His salvation in Christ, it's also the story about how God has been at work in your life day by day. And if God has been at work in your life, it is anything but boring. It is anything but dull. It is an exciting journey. It involves matters of the heart. Becoming a new creation in Christ means you are walking with God in every area of your life. Not an easy thing to do. Becoming a new creation in Christ can only happen by the work of the Holy Spirit. So do not think you can make the changes I am going to talk about in this book by your own willpower. Becoming a new creation in Christ only happens when you yield to the work of the Holy Spirit.

Maybe you have heard the phrase, "dead in the water." It may refer to a sailboat out on a lake or in the ocean when there is no wind. Dead in the water. No movement. No energy. Just waiting for something to happen. Frankly, that is how some people, if they are honest, would describe their Christian life. Dead in the water. The wind of the Spirit has not been filling their sails. They are just waiting for something to happen. It is interesting that the Greek word for the Holy Spirit is the word pneuma. That Greek word speaks of air or wind. We get the English word pneumatic from that Greek word. A pneumatic tool is powered by compressed air. If the Holy Spirit is not bringing to your life the wind of God to make you a new creation in Christ, you are, spiritually speaking, "dead in the water." You are not going anywhere. You are stuck in the ocean of life, waiting for something to happen. Does that describe you? Or are the sails of your spiritual life full of the power of the Spirit? Be sure of this, the Spirit of God can and will get you moving on the journey of becoming a new creation in Christ. But you need to be open to the work of God in your life.

Some years ago, my wife and I took our boat from the East coast of the State of Florida to the West Coast of Florida and met up with three of our four children to venture out into the Gulf of Mexico to do some fishing. Everything was going well, except for the catching of fish part, until about 11:00 a.m. As I moved the throttle forward in the boat to go to another fishing spot, nothing happened. The motor sped up. The boat did not move. Upon further inspection, it became obvious that we had spun a prop. In the propeller, there is a rubber hub that is either pressed into the prop or glued in. The prop had broken loose. We were about fifteen miles offshore. So, I decided to idle into the dock and see if the prop would hold at idle. It did until 5:00 p.m. We had idled for six hours! At that point, we were less than a mile from the dock. We could see the dock. But we could not move. Dead in the water. It was not a good feeling!

We tried to signal passing boats that we needed help. We waved life jackets, empty gas cans, almost anything to get the attention of other boaters. We used flares. We used a horn. Noone stopped. Dead in the water. One of my sons got the idea that if we tied a rope around him, he could manually swim the boat to the dock. I guess he thought he was an Olympic swimmer or Tarzan. When he tried to move the boat by swimming, he could not move the boat against the current and wind. So I tried it! Same result. Dead in the water. As the sun began to set, we called the coast guard on the radio. At least I did have a radio! The coast guard said they would contact a rescue company, Sea Tow, who would contact us to arrange a rescue. By that time, we all wondered if we were going to spend a night in the boat on the water. Dead in the water.

About that time, a miracle happened. A much smaller boat came up behind us. The driver of the boat said, "Do you need some help? Having any trouble?" We told him we were having trouble. He towed us into the dock. We canceled the mayday call to Sea Tow and made it into the dock. I tried to give the rescue boat driver some money. He refused it. He said, "It's what boaters do. Pay it forward some time to someone else who is in trouble." He saved me a great deal of money! When we were dead in the water, we met a Good Samaritan! Was that a God thing? I think so. Maybe this book will be God's rescue mission for you if you are feeling dead in the water spiritually. Maybe you need a God thing to happen in your life!

Are you dead in the water spiritually? Have you tried to solicit help from other people only to find they have their own agenda, their own issues, and are unwilling or unable to help? Have you tried to change things in your own power, only to find that you don't have what it takes to change? Have you reached out to some rescue expert, a doctor, pastor, counselor, only to realize that they are limited in what they can do? Let me be blunt. God knows where you are. God can send the resources that are needed to get you moving again. God does not want you to live "dead in the water" regarding your spiritual life.

It was while we were at my sister's house in Mississippi that I had a dream. In my dream, I was writing a book. I knew in my dream the title of the book and the chapters. The Scripture passage that I read in the dream was 2 Corinthians 5:17, "If anyone is in Christ, he is a new creation. The old is gone, the new has come." In my dream, I was writing about that passage! I had the chapters of this book given to me in that dream. I woke up at 3 a.m. I got up and began to write down that vision from my dream. I believe God was speaking to me in that dream. The basic content of this book was given to me in that dream. Yes, I believe God can and does give us insight in dreams. So, when I get writer's block, I go take a nap! Perhaps God has something to say to me in a dream! Just kidding. As I say to my wife sometimes, "I'm just messing with ya!" It is not wise to rely on dreams as the way to discern the counsel of God. God has given us the Bible. The Bible is God's revelation to us. The Bible is God speaking to us. Any dream we have cannot add to or negate the truth of God's Word. Our faith does not depend on dreams. Our faith depends on the truth of the Word of God. I do believe that God is involved in the process of writing this book, and therefore the truths shared in this book can be life-changing.

CHAPTER ONE

Becoming a New Creation Spiritually

God has created us as spiritual beings. This means we have a need and a desire to get to know a spiritual being, namely, God. The true God is Father, Son, and Holy Spirit. The true God is three persons united into one being. In theology, we call this unity of three persons into one God the Trinity. This unity of three persons in the Godhead is a mystery. We cannot fully comprehend it. As Christians, we accept the theology of the Trinity as a teaching of the Scripture and as an essential doctrine of the Christian faith. The only true God is Father, Son, and Holy Spirit. When we speak of spirituality, we are speaking about our relationship with the one true God.

We begin a relationship with the one true God when we are born again, that is when we are born spiritually. Once you have this relationship with God, either by receiving as a gift of God's grace the new birth in the waters of baptism or by trusting in Christ as your Savior from sin and death, you have the gift of eternal life in heaven. But during our time on this earth, we can either be close to God or be far from Him. We can grow in our relationship with God, or we can neglect our relationship with God. We can be sensitive to the Spirit of God, or we can stiff-arm the Spirit of God. We can walk in the Spirit, or we can walk in the flesh, that is, our sinful nature. We can care about spiritual things, or we can care more about the things of this world. We can have a strong love for God, or we can lose our love for God. We can know God intimately, or we can know things about God. There is a difference. To grow as a new creation in Christ means we grow deeper in our relationship with God. We are more aware of His presence in our life. We constantly yield to His will in our life. We are mindful of God every moment of our lives. We want to please God in how we live. So, how is it going in your relationship with God?

I think everyone who has received the gift of God's forgiveness through Christ and been made alive in Christ spiritually has experienced vibrant spiritual times as well as times where their spirituality has been lifeless and dull. I know I have. It is part of living in this fallen world that we will, at times, feel out of touch with God. This does not lesson the reality that God is there, that God loves us, and that God is still the same. Who God is, does not change. Our feelings change. But God does not change. We do not want to subject the truth about God to our feelings or to our reason. Frankly, there are some things about God that we will not be able to fully understand. How do you fully understand the Trinity? How do you fully understand eternity? How do you fully understand the fact that the Son of God, Jesus, died on the cross? We dare not make the truth of God dependent upon our reasoning or our feelings. If we do, God is no bigger than we are. I would prefer that God is different than us. Totally different. Therefore, there will be some things about God that we will not be able to fully understand. I am okay with that, and I hope you are too. Our spirituality is not so much defined by how much we know about God and the Bible but by how it is about a living relationship with God. Spirituality is about walking with God day by day.

It is interesting to compare our spirituality to the life-giving principles of water. Jesus told the woman at the well in John 4 that He could give her living water. The Holy Spirit is described as a spring of water in John 7. So spiritually speaking, a person can be parched, cracked, wilting, or dry like the desert if they are not being nourished with the life-giving Spirit of God. But if the Spirit of God is bringing the nourishing water of the grace and truth of God to a person's life, there will be life and growth. Unless the branches are connected to the nourishment of the vine, the branches will not grow (See John 15). The amount of connection you have in your life to the life-giving water of God will determine the level of your spirituality.

There have been times in my life when I have been too busy doing the work of God that I did not hear from God or connect with God. There are times in my life that I did not get quiet and get focused on God. When that happened, I began to wilt spiritually. There are times in my life when I walked away from God because I wanted to do what I wanted to do. If you consistently choose to quench the Spirit of God and go the way of disobedience to God, you will begin to dry up spiritually. There are times in my life when I let trouble, trials, and tribulations eclipse my faith in the greatness of God. The problems of life seemed bigger than the person of God. When that happens to you, you will begin to dry up spiritually. There are times in my life when I thought that the things of this world would meet my needs more than God would. I chased after things that could not deliver real peace or satisfaction. Just like plants and grass, if they do not receive enough water, they will wither and could possibly die. We are like that spiritually. If we do not receive the nourishment of the grace and truth of God, we will wither and possibly die spiritually. So, are you like the desert spiritually speaking? Or are you like a lush field? Is there new growth in your life, spiritually speaking?

I think it is difficult to grow spiritually when you are experiencing a lot of pain in your life. When you are in a lot of pain, you tend to focus on the pain, not on the Lord. We have all been there. There is a point in the time of pain when we reach the end of ourselves and want to cry out to God. It is at this moment that we realize our need for God and are ready for God to speak to us about our pain. But sometimes, the pain yells so loudly that God's voice seems to be drowned out. I remember when my mother died suddenly in 1996. She was only sixty-five years old, not much older than I am now. I felt a great deal of pain at her death. My children were young, and we had to break the news to them that their grandmother had died. My father was in shock and seemed to be, emotionally speaking, somewhere else. My mother's death brought all kinds of unanswered questions for me and for my siblings.

After my mother died, my wife asked me to go to the grocery store and buy some items on her shopping list. I did not know where all the items were in the store, so I had to hunt them down. I walked down one aisle in the store and saw a row of peanut butter and jelly jars. All of a sudden, I began to cry. As

I walked down that aisle, I reflected back on how my mother had made me peanut butter and jelly sandwiches as a child. I grieved. The mother who loved me enough to make those sandwiches was no longer on this earth. The care and love that the peanut butter and jelly aisle symbolized were to be no more in my life. In that aisle, I cried like a baby.

I was asked by my siblings to preach at my mother's funeral. That was tough. Probably the most difficult thing I have ever done in my life. I remember before the funeral thinking, what if heaven is not a real place? What if loved ones who die do not go to heaven? For a moment, I doubted all that I believed. I wondered if my mother lived beyond the grave. That was a terrifying moment for me. I was a pastor. I often spoke to grieving people at the death of their loved ones. I gave them the hope that there was truly life beyond the grave. You see, in the moment of intense pain, you tend to give up on what you have known all your life. This does not mean that you have lost your faith. It does not mean you are no longer a believer in Christ. It means that you are looking your pain in the eye, and you are having a difficult time with it. That is only human.

Thankfully, that moment of doubt lasted only for a brief time. No matter how much pain I felt, God was still God, and His truth was still the truth. I knew my mother believed in Jesus as her Savior. I knew that Jesus had promised eternal life to anyone who believed in Him as their Savior. I knew my mother passed from this life to the joys of heaven. It is not wrong to have a crisis of faith. What is wrong is to get stuck in that crisis of faith. If you have given up on God, come back to Him. Cling to His Word. Accept what is more important than your feelings, the Word of God. The Word of God will last forever. Your feelings will not last forever. What would you say is more important? Your feelings in the moment, or the Word of God that lasts forever? The choice is clear. We all struggle with our spirituality, but that struggle need not be the end of the story.

Some people think that they are made new spiritually by some kind of emotional experience. If they go to a conference and get saturated in worship, teaching and fellowship, they experience a spiritual high. They believe their faith is strong and that they can handle anything. They are relying on the feelings of the moment rather than on the objective truth of God's Word. There is nothing wrong with going to a conference to get pumped up spiritually. The problem is the effects of that weekend experience don't last. It is like eating a good meal. It satisfies at first, but if you are like me, you get hungry again a few hours later! There has to be something that lasts longer. The truth of the Word of God lasts forever. The power of the Word of God is available to us each and every moment. Becoming new creations in Christ involves feeding on the Word of God in our lives every day, not just at conferences.

Some people think they are made new spiritually when they spend time in nature. My wife and I went for a walk on the beach a few months ago. It was a beautiful day. The sound of the waves lulled away cares and anxiety. The sand between our toes created a comfortable cushion to connect us with the ground. It was a wonderful experience! Walking on the beach with my wife gave me a feeling of serenity and well-being. Walking on the beach reminded me that there is something bigger than myself, the God who created the ocean and all things, even husband and wife. But you cannot be at the beach all the time! If you can, get a life! There is nothing wrong with connecting with God in nature. All creation is a manifestation of His greatness. We need that from time to time. But there has to be something that sticks with us wherever we go and in whatever we are doing. We can experience that recreating experience of God every day as we become new creations in Christ.

Let me be clear about some theology. We become a new creation in salvation. That is what The apostle Paul is writing about in 2 Corinthians 5:17, "If anyone is in Christ, the new creation has come." We who were at one time dead in trespasses and sins have been made alive in Christ. The spiritual life that is found in Christ becomes imparted to us. Jesus is the way, the truth and the life (John 14:6). That life comes to us when we believe He is our Savior. The Bible calls this justification. Believing in Christ as Savior means God declares us to be "not guilty." We are forgiven of all our sins and born again spiritually. That is where the journey in a relationship with God starts. But it does not end there. There is also what we call sanctification. Sanctification is the process where we put to death the old sinful nature and become new creations in Christ. Sanctification is the process of becoming more holy. Becoming more like Christ is a life-long process. Sanctification is part of our response to the salvation won for us by Christ. Once we are saved, we want to please God. We want to become more like Christ. We want to be new creations in Christ.

It is possible to be involved in Christian things and not be serious about becoming a new creation in Christ. It is possible to be justified by faith but not to be sanctified on a daily basis by the Spirit of God. It is possible to be saved and not to grow spiritually. As a young person, I was raised in the church. I went to church every Sunday. I heard the Word of God preached. I went to Sunday School. But something was missing. I did believe Christ had saved me. I believed I would go to heaven when I would die. But my experience of Christ was a Sunday morning event. I did not walk with the Lord during the week. I lived for myself. Needless to say, although all the power of God was available for me to live a new life, I did not allow that power to change me and how I lived. The result? I was not a happy camper. I did not have the love, joy, and peace that the Holy Spirit wanted to give me. The times of real joy in my life were far and few between. Something was missing.

In my senior year of high school, I was invited by a youth leader in my church to attend the Florida-Georgia District of the Lutheran Church-Missouri Synod High School youth gathering. It was to be held at a retreat center north of Orlando, Florida. The gathering was to run from Friday evening until Sunday at noon. I did not want to go. A whole weekend singing songs and listening to sermons? Yuck. I was okay with my religion. So I thought. So I declined to go. I had two jobs and a girlfriend. Making money during that weekend and spending time with my girlfriend were both more important to me than spending a weekend at a retreat. I viewed going to a weekend retreat as a waste of time. Amazingly, in a similar way, some people think an hour on Sunday in worship and hearing the

Word of God preached is a waste of time! They are comfortable with their religion, or lack thereof. Other things are more important to them.

But the youth leader would not give up. Every time she saw me, she talked to me about going to this retreat. Each time she would talk with me about going to this retreat, I came up with some lame excuse. I told her I would have to work. I told her I wanted to take my girlfriend out on a date. I told her I was too busy. Finally, it was the week of the retreat. I thought I was home free. I thought I had convinced her that I was not going to this retreat. It was too late to register. I did not want to pay the hundred dollars to go. The deadline to register for the retreat has passed. After she pressed me again about going to that retreat, I shared my final objection. I said, "I cannot go on this retreat because I have not paid for the retreat." She said, "I already signed you up and paid for you to go." Gotcha! I had completely run out of excuses. I went to that retreat.

If you are praying for God to grab someone's heart and you keep getting a rejection, don't give up! Be loving, of course. But don't give up. Remember, love never quits. It has been said by salespeople that it takes seven requests or presentations before you get a "yes." Don't give up. If you are applying for a job and get a rejection, don't give up. If you care about a person's spiritual life, keep talking about your relationship with God. Don't nag. Don't badger the person who is not open to a relationship with God. Just keep sharing your experiences with God. Keep inviting them to open their heart to God. You never know what God can do in a person's life!

Well, I went to that youth retreat. I sat in the back seat of the youth counselor's car as we traveled to the retreat center, thinking to myself, What have you gotten yourself into? When we arrived at the retreat center, I saw there was about five hundred youth there. Interesting, I thought. There was singing. There was a skinny gray-haired pastor doing a teaching. Just what I thought. A weekend-long church service! I had had enough. So, I went outside, into the woods, sat down on a log, and began to smoke a cigar. I know. Not a good idea.

As I sat there in the darkness, I could hear the group singing in the background. All of a sudden, a man walked out of the woods. I know he could see me smoking the cigar, so I did not try to hide it. I thought, You are busted now. It is against the rules to use tobacco. You might be sent home. I could only be so lucky. The man walked up to me and said, "You are here for a reason. This is a place where God changes people's hearts and lives. You might want to think about that." With that, he turned around and went back into the woods. I had said nothing. I was dumbfounded that he did not scold me, report me, lecture me. It shocked me. That was the beginning of a God encounter for me. Who was that man? I looked for him the rest of the weekend but never saw him again. Was he an angel? I don't know if he was an angel, but he definitely brought me a message from God. That night I did not sleep very well. I wondered what was going on in my life. Why was I here at this place?

The next day I began to notice something. There was more to this retreat than singing and preaching. There were games and sports. I liked games and sports. The people I played with in the games were so loving. It did not matter to them whether you won or lost. The important thing was that each person felt special and valued. Strange, I thought. I began to feel that the youth at this retreat had something that I did not have. I noticed they actually enjoyed singing the songs and actually enjoyed hearing the pastor. I noticed that they enjoyed being with one another, encouraging one another, and were having a great deal of fun. I was not having fun, but they were. Why? Then it dawned on me that they had something I did not have. They had a living relationship with God. They really believed that God was there at that retreat and present in their lives. They had a love for God, and it showed in how they loved one another. I wanted that love. I wanted what they had. My heart began to melt. The walls I had erected so that I could do life my way began to come down. The door to my heart opened. And God came in.

When I came home from that retreat, my older brother realized something had happened to me. He said I was different. I did not understand it at the time, but what was different was that God had captured my heart. When I went to school the next Monday, I could not behave the way I used to behave. I realized that to say curse words hurt the God who loved me so much that He would die for me. The curse words could not come out of my mouth. I stopped hanging out with the people that before that time were my friends. I began to take a small pocket Bible to my classes and read it before class would start. I began to show love to people that, before that weekend, I did not care about. I had changed. This was a starting point on my journey to becoming a new creation in Christ. It was not something that I had done. It was the work of God by His Holy

Spirit. I realized that although God had changed me during that retreat, God was not done changing me. I was then open to that change. I hope you are too. You can teach an old dog new tricks! Young dogs too!

It is possible to have a new, fresh relationship with God anytime, anywhere. That is how we become new spiritually. In theology, we call it sanctification. It is the lifelong process of living out the love of God in our lives. How do you do that? It involves at least these four things.

First of all, it is important to admit our need for God. This is not as simple as it sounds. Our sinful pride is very strong. Sinful pride makes us think that we can do life all by ourselves without any intervention from God. Our sinful pride makes us believe we need God, but only a little bit of God. Not enough of God to really change our lives. After all, in our sinful pride, we think we are doing pretty good!

I will give you an example of sinful pride. Last November the stores were having a great sale on televisions. I made a sales pitch to my wife that a newer smart TV would be faster on the internet and that our daughter needed our old TV, plus there were some great sporting events coming up that would be much nicer on a sixty-five-inch TV rather than a forty-five inch TV. She agreed! What a salesman I am!

We bought the TV. When we got the TV home, there was a problem. How do you get this brand new big TV into the house? Could one person (that person being me) handle it? It seemed too big for my wife to help. But I was determined. I would carry the TV into the house. I can do it myself! Then she said it. I've heard what she said before, and I had the same reaction. She said, "Why don't you go ask one of the neighbors to help you?" Simple question. Simple request. When she said, "Why don't you go ask for help?" the hair on the back of my neck tingled. I shuddered. Ask for help? No way! I would rather die! I was determined to get that brand new sixty-inch TV in the house by myself! What's the problem here? The problem was not the TV. The problem was my pride. I can do it myself.

I got the same hair-raising feeling when my wife used to say to me, "Why don't you stop and ask for directions?" When she asked that, I would think, I have already asked for directions. I had prayed and asked God to show me where to go. What better source of guidance could you go to? God is better than Siri. God is better than AAA. God is better than Google Maps. So, why ask anyone else? The problem? Again, pride.

Why do men in particular refuse to go to the doctor? Here's why. They think whatever problem they have may just heal on its own. If that happens, there is no need for a doctor! Or, in a more spiritual sense, they may think they already asked God to take care of the physical problem! They may reason: If I have asked God, the great physician, why go to a doctor? There are also some logical excuses that men may use. Logical excuses like the symptoms may pass on their own. It will cost more money to go to a doctor. It will take my precious time to sit in a waiting room and then wait in an examination room, then wait for some tests, etc. You get the idea. What's the problem? Pride. Good old-fashioned ugly pride.

Sinful pride has been around since the beginning. God came to the first man, Adam, in the garden of Eden and asked,

"Did you eat the fruit from the tree that I told you not to eat fruit from?" (Genesis 2:11) God was not asking for information. He already knew the answer. He was gently asking the man to come clean. What did Adam say? It was the woman. She gave me the fruit, and I ate it. I am not culpable. What's the problem? Pride.

When Moses was up on the mountain to talk with God, the people of Israel got impatient that Moses had been gone so long. They thought Moses must have died on the mountain since he was gone for such a long time. They asked Aaron to make them some gods so they could have something tangible, visible, relatable to worship. So, Aaron took some of their gold and fashioned a calf. He made it with his own hands. The people thought it was great! Now we have a god that we can really relate to! They began to worship the golden calf. Enter Moses. He comes down from the mountain and sees what is going on. In effect, he says to Aaron, "What were you thinking?" Aaron's response is classic. He said, "I threw the gold in the fire and out jumped a calf" (Exodus 32:19-24). Well, if that had really happened, it must have been a God thing. But that is not what happened. Aaron lied. He fashioned the calf with his own hands. It was not a God thing. What is the problem here? Pride.

We are all prone to think we can handle things on our own. I can do it myself. With that way of thinking, you don't need God. Nothing can be further from the truth. Pride leads to firetruck faith. You think, *I will only call on God when there is a crisis. When the house is burning down, then I will call on God. When the doctor tells me that I have an incurable disease, then I will call on God. The rest of the stuff I can handle.* Pride. God resists that kind of attitude and that kind of person. In other words, that kind of person will not get very far with God. We are all, to some degree, that kind of people. If you want to have a new spiritual relationship with God, the first step is to admit that you need Him. The truth is, you need Him every second. You need His love every second. You need His guidance every second. You need His forgiveness every second. In a world full of lies, you need His truth every second.

To admit that we need God is humbling. When I was first married, I remember that I would not, could not, admit that I needed something from my wife. I would give her hints. When she would criticize me about something in our relationship, I would give her the look. You know, lifting the eyebrows and rolling your eyes. That was my hint that I had a need. I wanted to be respected and not criticized. When I wanted some affection, I would come up behind her and wrap my arms around her. When she did not catch the hint, I would shut down emotionally. It sounded so wimpy at that time for me to admit that I had needs. But I did have emotional needs and still do. I need my wife to respect me, understand me, listen to me, hold me, support me, forgive me, believe in me. If you are married and do not think that you need your spouse, then why be married? Should I go on? What about God? Do we need God? We need Him more than anyone. When you wake up in the morning, tell the Lord you need Him. When you leave the house and go to work, tell the Lord you need Him. When you are dealing with difficult situations in life, tell the Lord you need Him. When you are anxious about anything, tell the Lord you need Him.

The first step to a deeper spirituality is to admit your need for God. If you won't do that, or can't, you will end up stiff-arming God. Not a good position to be in. If you want to become a new creation in Christ, it is important to admit that you need Him! Desperately need Him!

As a pastor, I was expected to be able to solve every problem. I was expected to be able to walk on water, cross every stream, climb every mountain, say the right word at the right time to every person. I often admitted to people that I did not know what to do but that God did. No one has the right answer all the time. This expectation, whether it is created in the mind of the pastor or communicated by the people in their congregation, creates tremendous tension for pastors. The result is the Pastor will want to portray outwardly that they know what God wants. Inwardly the pastor knows, at least in some situations, they do not know what God wants. The problem comes when the pastor portrays outwardly that they know the will of God, but inwardly they know they don't know the will of God. They end up playing the pastor game. They portray they are spiritual when inwardly they know they are not spiritual. It is normal to do this sometimes. This should only happen infrequently.

You can also play the Christian game. The Christian game is to portray that you know what God wants when, in reality, you do not know what God wants. You may portray outwardly that you are close to God when, in reality, you are far from God. You may know what the right answers are, but your heart is not connected to what you know. If playing the pastor game or the Christian game becomes your normal operating procedure, you are in trouble. Big trouble! What you need is what is known as a "come to Jesus" moment. Pastors can become so busy doing the work of God that they don't have time to connect with God.

I have been there. Let me tell you, it is not pretty to portray outwardly what is not real in your spirit. It feels fake, and it is fake! If this is where you are at, whether you are a pastor or not, get alone with God. Block out all the distractions of the TV, internet, family, and other distractions. Get silent before God and cry out to Him. Tell Him that you are done relying on your own power. Ask God to quench your parched spirit with the truth of His love and grace. We need God. We need His help. We need to trust God. We do not have all the answers for everything in our lives. Sometimes we will only realize our need for God when we reach the end of our resources. When we get to the point that we are desperate. When we don't know what to do. This is when you reach the point in your life where you realize that you cannot handle everything in your life in your own power and realize that you need someone who can help you deal with life. Then you will be open to the work of God in your life. You will be able to see that there is only one person who can help you. That person is God. Admit that you need God to work in your life. If you don't do this, you will end up stiff-arming God and keeping Him at a distance. You will not grow spiritually. You will not grow in being a new creation in Christ.

The second step is to get a vision check. If you have spiritual myopia, you will not see God at work in your life or in the lives of others. Myopia is the medical term for nearsightedness. People with myopia see objects more clearly when they are close to the eye, while distant objects appear blurred or fuzzy. Spiritual myopia is when you can see God when He reveals Himself very clearly in a given situation, but you cannot see Him when He seems distant.

In the Gospel of Luke, chapter 24, you have a post-resurrection appearance of Jesus. It is Easter afternoon. Two guys are walking away from Jerusalem. They are sad... downcast. They had just seen Jesus arrested, tried in an illegal court, brutalized, crucified, and buried in a tomb. As Jesus comes up to them as they are walking on the road, it appears Jesus knows they are having a bad day. So Jesus comes up beside them and asks what they have been talking about. Their answer betrays their spiritual myopia. "Are you the only one who has not heard about what has just happened in Jerusalem? They crucified Jesus. We had hoped he was the one to redeem Israel." Here is Jesus, the one who was killed, only a few hours later, walking with them! But they did not see it. They were blind to the presence of Jesus. They were blind to His resurrection. The answer to their sadness was right there in front of them. The same thing is true for us in every situation of our lives. The thing that will change everything is right there! It is Jesus. These two men walking on the road don't see Jesus. They don't see that Jesus is right there with them. They don't see how God was at work in their life right at that moment. Only when Jesus was at dinner with them and broke bread with them were their eyes opened (Luke 24:13-31). How often do we go through life wanting to see how God is working, but we are blind to it? Indeed, the second key to being a new creation spiritually is to develop the ability to see God in every situation of our lives. He is there. He is at work. He loves us that much!

During my first year in college, I came home on a break. My sister's glasses were sitting beside me on a lampstand in the family room. I decided to play around a little and picked them up and put them on. I looked around the room. I was able to read the book titles on the bookshelf. I asked, "Are you supposed to be able to see the book titles from here?" My sister laughed and recommended that I get my eyes checked. I attributed the degradation of my eyesight to studying the languages of Greek and Latin. That will do it to anyone! Needless to say, that led to an eye appointment with a Doctor and, yes, glasses.

If God appears to be far away, your vision of Him will be fuzzy at best. God is near. God is at work in the circumstances of your life. God is also with us in the time of temptation. He knows when we are being put to the test. He will provide a way out. But we won't take the way of escape if we do not see Him at work in the situation.

It makes sense that since God created everything as a manifestation of His glory, that spiritual truth can be seen in the things God has made. It makes sense that since God's truth is so relevant and life-giving, that His truth can be seen in almost every situation in our lives. In the Old Testament, David was a shepherd. Possibly one day, he was leaning on his staff and staring at some sheep. He began to think about God. Then it dawned on him, God is like a shepherd! God is the perfect shepherd! It is no coincidence that Jesus described Himself as the Good Shepherd! Read about that in John 10. David wrote Psalm 23 because he could see God as a shepherd. Psalm 23 has a whole list of things God does for us as the Good Shepherd! The truth is, in your life, figuratively speaking, you can see silly, smelly sheep, or you can see God at work in your life. It all depends upon your spiritual sight.

The apostle Paul did the same thing in a prison cell. He was chained next to a Roman soldier. He started to see some spiritual truths about God. You can read about it in the book of Ephesians, chapter 6. Paul saw truth about God in the armor of a Roman soldier! Jesus did this all the time. Many of His parables are all about using common ordinary things to teach spiritual truth. If something is going on in your life, God is there, and if you can see Him, you will be profoundly affected. Can you see God in the ordinary things of life? Can you see God in your temptations? Can you see God in your trials?

It is possible to see truth about God in the ordinary things of life. I have given many children's messages over the years. Children's messages are short teachings about some spiritual truth using a common ordinary everyday object. What I have realized is that almost anything can be used as a spiritual example if you can see spiritual truth involved. One of my favorite children's messages is to use a hammer and a pipe wrench. I introduce the hammer and the wrench to the children as Harold Hammer and Wendy Wrench. Harold Hammer and Wendy Wrench live in Never Sorry Land. Harold Hammer hits people. Wendy Wrench has a big mouth and says unkind things to people. One time, when Wendy's dog snapped at Harold, Harold hit the dog. At that point, I hit the wrench with the hammer. When Wendy saw Harold hit the dog, she yelled at him and called him names. I wave the pipe wrench, opened wide as can be, at the hammer. Harold did not like to be called names, so he hit Wendy. Again, I hit the pipe wrench with the hammer. Wendy yelled at Harold, telling him he was a no good, bad person. (That is, putting it mildly.) Again, I wave the wrench at the hammer. Wow! Harold hits, and Wendy has a big mouth! I explain that sometimes this happens in relationships. Sometimes people injure other people, either physically or verbally, when they do not like what is going on. Sometimes people say things with their mouths that injure others.

When we feel injured by someone, we can respond in unkind ways that only make the situation worse. We can sometimes be like Harold Hammer and strike out at others. We can be like Wendy Wrench and say unkind things to others. We can live in Never Sorry Land. When we lash out at others, the hurt escalates. One thing that can change this escalation of hurt in our relationships is to simply say, "I am sorry." If Wendy had told Harold she was sorry her dog snapped at him, hoping he would not have hit the dog! I ask the children to practice saying, "I'm sorry." It is really not that difficult to say, "I am sorry." But it can change the whole course of a relationship. A hammer and wrench can teach profound spiritual truth if you see how God can use them. You can become new creations in Christ each day if you can see Him at work in your life and in the ordinary circumstances of life.

During my fourth year of studies at the seminary, I worked for a roofing company laying shingles in order to pay our bills. My wife and I had only been married less than two years. One week before Thanksgiving, I was working on a roof. It was cold and snowing. To start the roof, my co-worker and I put up a scaffold on the fascia board of the roof. We could then load the scaffold with shingles and start laying the first row of shingles on the roof. The fascia board was old and rotten. When the fascia board broke, the scaffold went under the rafters and wiped us off the scaffold. We fell to the ground. I managed to get my feet underneath me, hoping that my feet and legs would break my fall. I ended up dislocating my little toe on one foot, breaking three bones in that foot, and turning my ankle on the other foot. The foreman for the roofing company was called. He took me to a nearby clinic. They took x-rays. The doctor told me that he could not do anything for my foot, that I needed to see an orthopedic specialist. I was taken to a specialist. He looked at the x-rays and said that he could set the bones in my foot manually, or he could set them in surgery. He gave me the choice. I decided for him to set the bones manually. It was not fun, but it worked! I walked with crutches for a couple of weeks.

Here is how God worked in the situation. When I became injured, I started receiving a regular check from Workman Comp. I continued to receive those checks to the end of March after the winter weather broke and I could return to work. I did not work from Thanksgiving until almost Easter, but I got paid! It dawned on me that God did not want me doing roofing during that winter. Sure, I did not like injuring my foot and ankle, but God was at work even during the recuperation time to provide us with an income.

What current situation are you going through in your life? Can you see God at work in the situation? Sometimes it takes time to see how God is a work. Can you see by faith that God is at work in the difficult situations of your life? Becoming a new creation in Christ spiritually means you trust that God is at work whether you see it or not. Becoming a new creation in Christ means you see more and more how God is at work in your life.

The third key to becoming a new creation spiritually is to fall in love with God every day. Falling in love with God on a daily basis does not happen automatically. Knowing that God loves you takes no work at all. All you do is look at the cross and realize that He did something for you that no one else could do. He died for you. God so loved you that He gave His only begotten Son into death for your salvation. The cross is the story of God's love for you. But staying in love with God each day takes work. It is like a marriage relationship. If you want to keep your marital love fresh, it takes a lot of work! If you neglect your marriage relationship, the feelings of love will grow cold.

This can also happen in your relationship with God. If you neglect your relationship with God, your love for God can grow cold. Remember in the Book of Revelation, Jesus looks at the church in Ephesus and says, "You have lost your first love" (Revelation 2:4). It is possible in our relationship with God to grow cold in our love for God. It can happen in a marriage relationship. Your love for your spouse can grow cold if you let that happen. During marriage counseling, I heard about love in marriage growing cold. People would tell me that they love their spouse, but they are not in love with them. What they mean is that they are committed to the relationship, but the feeling of closeness and passion has grown cold. How did that happen? They took their relationship for granted. They allowed the normal tasks of life to become more important than their relationship. They stopped doing the things that keep a relationship strong. They have allowed hurt in the relationship to overcome their feelings of love. Have you done that with the Lord? How can you change it?

If you have been on a trip or away from a loved one for a period of time, when you get back together, you renew the relationship. You catch up. You bond again. You give focused attention to one another. In that moment, nothing else matters. You give undivided attention to your relationship. Love, like a fire, can be stoked. If you leave a fire alone or neglect it, it will grow cold. It will smolder. A fire, like love, may even burn out if you neglect it long enough. That can also happen in your relationship with God. It can happen spiritually.

Here are some things we can do to cultivate intimacy with God:

Set a date night. Plan for special times when you focus only on God and growing in love with Him. You can do this by reading the Bible. The Bible is God's love letter to you. The Bible is God's bid for connection. In the Bible, God approaches you and says, "Hey, do you care enough about our relationship to get together? Will you do that with just Me and you?" Set a date with the Lord and focus on Him. Listen to what He has to say to you.

Schedule some intimate times with the Lord. When a couple gets intimate with one another, they are very vulnerable. They open up to one another. They give of themselves to one another. Spiritually speaking, think of this as prayer. In prayer, you open your heart to God. You pour out your hopes and dreams to Him. You listen to Him share Himself with you. Listen, if your prayer time with the Lord is sweet, if it is a time when you can be intimate with God, you will want to pray!

The fourth way to be a new creation spiritually is to celebrate the Lord. Jesus said one time the greatest commandment is to "Love the Lord with all your heart, soul and mind." (See Matthew 18 and Mark 11.) Most Bible teachers will say this passage means to love the Lord with all your being! That is a good start, but what does it really mean? The Greek word for heart is cardia. It is where we get the word cardiologist. It means to love passionately. It means you put your heart into it. You feel something. You choose to feel love for the Lord and not for anyone else. The truth is you get excited about what is important to you. To love the Lord with all your heart means you celebrate who the Lord is. You are excited that He loves you! You get excited about His truth. You get excited about His promises. You get excited about what He has done for you. Celebrate what you have been through together. Celebrate what He has done for you. Celebrate who God is. Celebrate what He will do for you in the future. Love Him for that!

Wedding anniversaries and birthdays are times to celebrate people and the relationship we have with them. Many years ago, I took a week's vacation and went to Boy Scout Camp with two of my sons in North Carolina. It was great! To be with my sons in the mountains was a great joy. We arrived home late Saturday night. I was to preach and teach Bible class the next day, which I did. After the second service, I was ushered into our fellowship hall, where there was a huge gathering of people. My wife had secretly put together a surprise birthday party for me! Some of my siblings were there. My children were there. I got roasted royally, all in good fun. We all had a great time! You know, what amazed me was that people really wanted to be there! They wanted to celebrate! Their hearts were in the celebration. So, when is the last time you celebrated the Lord? If you truly want to celebrate the Lord, you will want to be in worship. You will want to gather with other people and celebrate who God is and what He has done. That is part of loving the Lord with all your heart.

The Greek word for soul is the word psyche. We get the word psychology from that word. It refers to your basic bent or personality. You have a unique way to love other people. No one loves my wife like I love her. I am kind and gentle, well, most of the time! I give her who I am. I will do things for her that I will not do for other people. To love God in this way is to give Him your soul. To have a special relationship with Him that you don't have with anyone else. It is a private love that only the two of you know and share. You enjoy this kind of love because you feel totally accepted for who you are. And you accept God for who He is.

To love God with all your mind means that you only think wonderful, beautiful things about Him. You hold Him in high positive regard. It means you love to think about Him because of who He is. When you fix your mind on the Lord, it lifts you above all that is negative and hurtful in this world. Loving God with your mind is your safe place. God is a "Father to the fatherless" (Psalm 68:5). God is a safe place to the fatherless. No matter what is going on in your life, if you love God with your mind, you will be mindful of God and find your safe place in God. God loves you with His whole mind! God has you in mind constantly. God wants the best for you. God understands you completely yet loves you unconditionally. Who wouldn't want to love a person like that?

Tell God you love Him. When we speak something, we commit to it. I tell my wife every day, often many times a day, that I love her. That is a blessing to her, and I need to say it. Saying it affirms it. Saying it helps me to be committed to it. Saying "I love you" takes the love from our heart and makes it known, audible, real. How many times a day do you tell the Lord that you love Him? Even if you don't feel it, say it. Commit to it. You may be going through a very difficult time in your life, and you don't feel that God loves you. You may not feel that you love God. Tell God you love Him anyway. Make a choice to express your love to God. You may be worshiping at church and singing a song about your love for God. You may not feel like you love God at that moment. Tell God you love Him in your song. Sometimes we feel pretty numb when it comes to our relationship with God, or for that matter, with other people. Telling God that we love Him can jump-start our feelings. Don't go by your feelings. Tell God you love Him because you know that is the right thing to do. When you tell God you love Him, it is amazing how our feelings will follow what we declare.

Lastly, you become a new creation in Christ when you enjoy the Lord. The apostle Paul said, "Rejoice in...in what?...in the Lord" (Philippians 4:4). Being with God and loving God is a good thing. It is a really a good thing. You find joy in what you value as good. Taste and see that the Lord is...good! (Psalm 34:8)

One rule of exercise is that if you don't enjoy the kind of exercise you are doing, you won't do it very long. I do not like running. Running hurts my body and is boring. I do like racquetball! I can get a workout playing racquetball that does not even seem like a workout! In the same way, spiritually speaking, if you dread going to church, spending time in prayer, or reading the Bible, you will have to force yourself to do it. How do you enjoy it? Simple. You see how these things meet a need for you. You need love, and God has perfect love for you. You need to serve something bigger than yourself. There is nothing bigger than God! You need to be understood. God understands you and loves you just as you are. You need security. God keeps His eye on you and is working all things together for your good (Romans 8:28). We do everything we do, good or bad because we have a need. God is the answer to your needs. So why not do what you do so that God can meet your needs? So simple, but so hard to do on a consistent basis. God is ready, willing, and able to meet your needs. Go to Him and enjoy letting Him love you!

Love God from the heart. That is the heart of the matter when it comes to growing spiritually. I ask you to apply the principles in this chapter to your life. Be honest with your answers.

1. How is it going in your heart, spiritually speaking? Are you dead in the water? Are you like the desert or a fertile field, spiritually speaking? When Has God manifested His presence in your life? What steps of growth would you mark on your spiritual growth chart?

2. Do you need God? Really need God? Do you see God at work in your life? Really see God at work?

3. Do you love God? Really love God with your whole heart? Do you say often that you love God? Do you tell God you love Him?

4. Do you find joy in God? Really find joy in God's goodness? You can! Do you celebrate who God is and what He has done in your life? How do you do that?

These things are vital to becoming a new creation in Christ spiritually. I appeal to you, open your heart to growing spiritually in God's love and grace.

CHAPTER TWO

Becoming a New Creation in Your Thinking

What we think about and how we think and process life in our minds has a great deal to do with what we do and why we do the things we do. It is very important to becoming a new creation in Christ to evaluate our thoughts and to control our thoughts. That is what we are going to look at in this chapter. Our thoughts are powerful indicators of where we are spiritually and what will be the outcome of our lives.

One Sunday after worship, I noticed a woman sitting in a pew crying. I asked her if she would like to talk. She said yes. So, we went to a room where our discussion could be more private. She told me her husband was seeing another woman. Not just seeing her, he was spending half of the weeknights with this other woman. When his wife would come to church, he would show up at church, sit next to her, and act like nothing was wrong. At the time, this couple had two young children. I asked the man to meet with me so that we could talk. When I told him what his wife had told me, he said, "It works for me, so why doesn't it work for my wife?" Somehow in his mind, he thought what he was doing just fine. Isn't it amazing how our thinking can sometimes get distorted? I told him God had a word for what he was doing. God called it adultery. Needless to say, after some counseling and his unwillingness to change, the marriage ended. Our thoughts have profound consequences, for good and for bad. The process of dealing with our thoughts is very important to becoming new creations in Christ.

The average person has between 25,000 and 60,000 thoughts a day! Just that thought is exhausting! Of those 25,000 to 60,000 thoughts during just one day, we make about 35,000 choices. I am not going to explain all the science behind these numbers because those who research this topic can't agree on what the real numbers are! So, let's take these numbers as a likely probability. What do you think about that? There, you just added another thought! The point is that our brains are very active each day and sometimes each night. Yet, we are not the helpless slaves of our thoughts. We can decide which thoughts we will focus on and which thoughts we will dismiss or discard. This process is very important to becoming a new creation in Christ. Some thoughts are irrational, sinful, destructive, or false and need to be discarded. Some thoughts are good and beneficial and need to be kept and explored. Becoming a new creation in Christ involves sifting through the thoughts that you have. Some thoughts we have come from our sinful flesh. Those thoughts need to be identified and replaced with Godly thoughts. If we want to become new creations in Christ, it is very important that we sift through our thoughts.

In Colorado, you can stop off the highway and pan for gold. At these tourist stops, there is steam of water flowing down a trough. You are given a pan that has a screen at the bottom of it. You simply pick up some of the soil and let the water sift out the soil to see what remains. I found when I did this that what remained were rocks, not gold. We were sifting out what was of no use and trying to find what was really valuable. The same is true in our thoughts. We need to sift out what is bad and seek to discover what is valuable and good. It is important if we want to become new creations in Christ that we identify and discard thoughts that are not of God and therefore are unhealthy. It is important that we replace these unhealthy thoughts with thoughts that please God and are therefore healthy. This is not an easy task. Sifting through our thoughts and changing negative thoughts to healthy thoughts is a life-long task. Just because we think something, does it follow that this thought is good or healthy? We are constantly in the process of sifting through our thoughts.

God knows that our thoughts become who we are. As a person thinks in their heart, so they are (Proverbs 23:7). Our thoughts chart the course of our lives. We can take control over our thoughts. We are encouraged in the Bible to take every thought captive to the obedience of Christ (2 Corinthians 10:5). God wants to help us discard bad thoughts and cultivate good thoughts. That is how we become new creations cognitively. We think God's thoughts. We take every thought captive to the obedience of Christ. Our thoughts are the real battleground of our lives. Other people, generally speaking, do not know what we are thinking all the time. God knows what we are thinking all the time. God wants to help us make some decisions about our thoughts and take control of them.

A person can get out of bed in the morning and have some depressive thoughts. They may think about their day and how they dread some of the people or things they will have to deal with during the day. They may look at the weather and think their day will not go very well if it is rainy, cloudy, or cold. They may choose to focus their thoughts on every physical pain they have. The result of focusing your mind on what is negative is you can think yourself into a bad day. If you continue to allow these negative thoughts, you may even begin to feel ill. You may begin to believe that God has somehow forgotten about you.

On the other hand, you can replace those depressive thoughts with more positive ones. You can choose to believe that God will help you with whatever situation you will face that day. You can choose to thank God for the rain because it is the way God waters the earth and makes plants grow. You can choose to thank God that you have a heated house if it is cold outside. If you think negative thoughts, your body will begin to manifest what coincides with your thoughts. If you think positive, faith-filled thoughts, your body will respond to those thoughts accordingly.

It is a constant battle to sift through our thoughts. I will give you an example from my own life. A couple of years ago, my wife and I went to Disney World. Disney World is only about an hour drive from our house. My wife wanted to arrive at Disney World the moment the gates opened. I thought, Why? I know she wanted to stay there all day. I thought, This will be a long, long day. Even though someone gave us free passes to

Disney, I still had to pay for parking. It is expensive to park at Disney! The lines for each ride at Disney were horrible. Some of the rides and displays had very long lines, so long that we did not wait to go into them. Why would you wait an hour to get into a ride when the ride only lasts twelve minutes? There were people all around us who were speaking languages that I did not understand. It was hot. Summer in central Florida. Know what I mean? When we wanted to get something to eat, there were lines. When I paid the bill, I thought, *What is so special about a hamburger that it costs twelve dollars?* It was not a special hamburger. At about 8 p.m, I was done. I was ready to go home. But the fireworks did not start until after 9 p.m. If we stayed for the fireworks, we would still need to get to the parking lot and drive home. You get the picture.

Here's the point. We were at the 'greatest place on earth,' and I had determined to have a no-good, rotten day only because of my thoughts. I had a choice. I could enjoy the moment, being with my wife, watching the people, marveling at the trimmed plants and the quaint streets, or I could focus on the hardships of the whole event.

How would God want me to think about that day at Disney World? I could have been grateful that we were able to gain entrance to Disney World, and it only cost us the parking fee. I could have seen the whole event as a way to minister to my wife and to make her happy. I could have been thankful for the exercise, all that walking. I could have thought about people who travel across the world to come to this theme park, and here I only had to drive one hour. I could have been thankful that I was healthy enough to even go to Disney World! But no!

That is not what I was thinking that day at Disney World. That is what can happen if we let our sinful, self-centered nature rule our thoughts rather than the Spirit of God.

As I write this, many people are on house arrest because of the Corona Virus. If you are an introvert, you may actually love being on house arrest! You don't have to deal with people, except maybe your family or virtually. Again, during a lock-down, you can focus your mind on all the negatives, or you can focus on the positives. You can be distressed that you are on a lock-down, or you can enjoy a change in your regular schedule to have some time with loved ones or time at home. It all depends upon your thinking.

When I visit people who are in prison, I tell them, first of all, that because they messed up and broke the law, there is a price to pay...jail time. Although the justice system is not very forgiving, God is! God has already provided forgiveness. God already took care of their wrongs when Christ died on the cross. They have already been pardoned by the most important person, namely, God. Therefore, the important thing for them to realize is that they can be free in their spirit by the grace of God even though they are not free to roam about society.

I also tell them that their time in prison need not be wasted time. God can use their time in prison to make them new creations! God knows where they are. God has promised to be with them wherever they go. God is with them in prison, and God has not given up on them. God can do life-changing work in their life while they are in prison if they will let Him. I encourage them to find Christian believers in prison and have fellowship with them. I suggest that they read the Bible and ask God to teach them what He wants to teach them. I tell them to develop some kind of skill while they are incarcerated so that when they get out of prison, they can do something more productive with their lives. Being in jail is not wasted time if God is at work during that time, making them a new creation in Christ.

Being at a job that is difficult is not wasted time if God is at work making you a new creation in Christ. Being in a marriage that is difficult is not wasted time if God is at work making you a new creation in Christ. When you think about other people in your life, do you tend to be too critical of them? Everyone has their weak points. None of us are perfect. If you want to think negatively about someone, I am sure you can find some things to support your case. You may even begin to think things about them that are not even true. Just as everyone has their weak points, they also have their strong points. In your thoughts, find the good in other people and focus on those thoughts. Let God take care of their weak points. By the way, God can do a better job of dealing with those weak points than you can! Waiting for healing from some kind of physical ailment is not wasted time if God is making you a new creation in Christ. It all depends on your thinking.

Identify thoughts that lead you down a path that is destructive to your life. No one can do this 100 percent of the time. We all mess up when it comes to dealing with our destructive thoughts. But God wants to help us. Those who walk according to the Spirit have their minds set on what the Spirit desires (Romans 8:5). It is amazing to me how some people know the Word of God, can quote Scripture, have been to numerous Bible studies, yet get stuck in negative, destructive thought patterns.

There are at least four destructive thought patterns. Let's look at each one of them.

One destructive thought pattern is obsessing about things that we really need to let go. When we obsess about things that we can do nothing about, that is a recipe for negative thinking. When we want to play God, we take over God's job. There are some things that happen in life where we want to play God. We want to control a situation and the outcome of the situation. We may want to justify our sinful behavior. We play God when we want to be right all the time and prove other people are wrong. We want to be the judge, jury, and prosecuting attorney. We would do well sometimes to let God be God and to trust Him with the outcome. As a recent song says, "Let it go!"

By the way, usually, when you obsess about something, you magnify the impact of it way beyond what is normal or is necessary. Are you thinking about some situation in your life, morning, noon, and night? If you do that for days, you know you have a problem. You are obsessing about the problem. People can obsess about the economy. You probably can't do much to change the economy. People can obsess about politics. You probably can't do much to change political outcomes. People can obsess about the weather. That's God's job too. Focus on something else. Focus on being grateful. When it rains, focus on how God is growing the plants. When a hurricane hits our area in Florida, I thank God that He is pruning the trees. When you are in pain, thank God that you are still breathing. When a governmental election does not go your way, focus on the fact that God has a plan for the ages, that our country is very large, and has many facets that keep it going. Think about how we as a nation have made it through many elections and have still survived as a nation. Focus on God being in control and working everything together for your good (Romans 8:28). Easily said but hard to do all the time. We can only be grateful in difficult situations if we are becoming new creations in Christ. Do not allow day-to-day problems control your thoughts or life. Get a larger, more eternal perspective. Obsessing about problems is a sign you want to be in control. Do what you can about the problem and leave the outcome up to God.

Early in my ministry, I visited a woman whose husband had died. Both of them had retired from their jobs years before the husband died. Her husband was not a member of the church, nor did he attend church. The wife had been a nurse. As her husband was dying of cancer, she took care of him. Really good care. They had many talks as he lay in the bed dying. She recorded these talks on cassette tapes. I am dating this story now! When I met with her after her husband had died, she was in her kitchen with a box of those tapes. She listened to them each day, a good part of the day. And she cried. She was stuck in her grief. She was fixated on the fact that her husband had died, and she was now a widow. She was obsessing over the loss of her husband and their marriage. She could even justify this obsessing by thinking it was the loving thing to do. But it was not healthy. It was blocking her recovery from grieving. Her husband was still alive in her, thinking if she could hear him every day on those cassette tapes. I said to her that what she was doing to herself by listening to those cassettes was not good for her. I asked her to give me the tapes for a month. That was a huge decision for her. Those tapes were her lifeblood! I said I would keep them for a month, then give them to her son, who could, at his discretion, give them back to her. She needed a change in thinking. She needed to release her husband to God's eternal care. She needed God to give her a new perspective on the death of her husband in order to be a new creation in Christ. She agreed to give me the tapes. What was I doing by taking those tapes from her? I was forcing her to change her thinking.

What tapes are you playing over and over in your mind? What are you clinging to for hope and security? There is only one thing that gives hope and security in the changes of life, God Himself. Cling to Him! Listen to the recorded Word of God!

Another destructive thinking pattern is to nurse hurts. We all get hurt by others. There is a reason for that. Being hurt by others is the result of sin, and all of us are sinners. Sin causes hurt in our relationships. Think of the emotional hurt you feel in your heart like the hurt you feel when you have a physical wound. If you have a scratch on your arm and keep picking at it every day, the scratch will not heal. It will only get worse. Have you ever scratched a bug bite to get some relief from the itching and find that the itching does not go away? Keep scratching at that bug bite, and you will have a sore that can become infected! The same thing can happen with our emotional wounds. If you keep thinking about the hurt you feel in your relationships, you will discover that the hurt grows; it does not diminish.

If you have been hurt by someone, don't keep going over the hurt in your mind! Go to the divine healer. God is a mender of broken, wounded hearts. Give the hurt to Him. By the stripes of Christ, we are healed, not only of our sin but also our emotional hurts (1 Peter 2:24). Forgive the one who hurt you, whether they deserve forgiveness or not. Forgive them whether they admit they have hurt you or not. Forgive, as God, for Christ's sake, forgives you (Ephesians 4:32). When you forgive someone, you think differently about the person who hurt you. You love them and want to minister to them. When you forgive the hurt, you release the person who hurt you of any debt you feel they may owe you. They do not owe you anything for the hurt they have caused you because you have already released any debt they may owe you. You have given them the gift of forgiveness. This is a difficult thing to do. Only by the grace of God can we do this. Only as we become new creations in Christ can we truly forgive the hurts other people cause in our lives.

If you have a family member that hurt you in the past and you, don't want to have anything to do with them now or in the future, you are nursing a hurt. If you leave a church because you did not get your way regarding some issue in the church, you are nursing a hurt. If you loaned someone some money and they never paid you back, and you can't get the debt out of your mind, you are nursing a hurt. If you treat someone poorly because of how they treated you in the past, you are nursing a hurt. If Jesus could forgive his accusers and executioners on the cross, you can forgive those who hurt you. While being crucified on the cross, Jesus said, "Father, forgive them, for they do not know what they are doing" (Luke 23:34). Forgiving others who have hurt us involves being a new creation in Christ. Let God execute justice at the appropriate time! God can do a much better job at it than you! (Romans 12:19)

A third destructive thought pattern is narrow thinking. We like to be in control. One way we feel in control is to define our perfect view of how something should be and what it should not be. When we do this, we feel justified in our viewpoint that our thinking is the right way to handle something and, therefore, the only way. Wrong. Wrong. Wrong. If you are too subjective in your thoughts, you will not be able to take into account the viewpoint of others. Guess what? Other people will often have a different viewpoint than you do! Narrow thinking people are not good listeners. Their mind is already made up! And if you don't fit in their preconceived view of the way things should be, then you are viewed as being wrong. When other people do not agree with us, it is important to ask whether there is a principle or truth of Scripture that is at stake. Be careful here. Some people have justified all sorts of dysfunctional things on the basis of some Scriptural truth. If there is a Scriptural principle at stake, seek to draw the other person to that principle. If there is not a clear Scriptural principle at stake, it may be that the two of you just have opposite opinions! It is wise to have this mindset: other people may not be wrong, just different. By the way, married couples would do well to remember this adage when it comes to the inherent differences in how men and women think. Sometimes my spouse is not wrong, just different!

It is not wrong that my wife likes to go shopping and I don't like to go shopping. Not wrong, just different. It is not wrong when I want to go somewhere at the agreed-upon time, but my wife often has things to do at the last minute that push us past that time. Not wrong, just different. It is not wrong for me to feel that I can drive for hours without saying anything when my wife wants to talk during that time as a way to connect. Not wrong, just different. It is not wrong for me to want to be by myself for a period of time when she wants to be together. Not wrong, just different. It is not wrong for me to want to connect sexually with my wife when she wants to do some sewing or some work on the computer. Not wrong, just different.

Be careful here. Some people just do whatever they want with no regard for their partner. They may even get upset when their partner challenges their decisions. You could instead say in your thoughts, they are not wrong, just different. But if the relationship suffers, being different can be wrong. If we focus more on our right to do what we want and don't compromise for the sake of the relationship, the relationship can be damaged.

I know a man who went golfing after work almost every day. That meant he was not home for supper with the family and golfed until the sun began to set. He went golfing on Saturdays. He went golfing after church on Sunday. He was good at golf. His wife did not like to golf. It was not wrong for him to golf once in a while. The times he would golf should have been negotiated with his wife. It was wrong for him to spend so much time golfing because golfing was more important to him than time with his wife and family. They had different interests and by not negotiating those differences for the sake of their relationship, what he ended up doing was hurtful to his marriage and family. This husband and wife were different when it came to golf, but it was wrong for him to make golf more of a priority than his wife and children. It seemed to me that since his wife didn't make a big deal about him being gone playing golf so much, maybe she enjoyed not having him around the home!

Some people think there is a narrow way of eating. They may think that to eat pork is wrong. Some people think that to eat meat cooked on a grill is wrong. They reason: meat cooked on a grill can cause cancer! Some people even say to eat meat is wrong! That is narrow thinking. It can lead to a critical, judgmental viewpoint of others. We have the freedom in Christ to make our own choices. We fall into narrow thinking when we take that freedom away from other people and seek to control their choices.

Some people think that there is only one way to worship. Some people think the music in worship has to be fifteenth-century hymns and ancient liturgy. That is narrow thinking. Some people think the music has to be the most contemporary songs with clapping and lifting of hands. Any other way to worship is lifeless and wrong. That is narrow thinking. Let me say it: God is not so much interested in the way we worship, as He is interested in our heart as we worship.

Some people may think their spouse needs to be so godly that they pray for an hour every day, read the Bible for an hour every day, never get angry or upset, and always do the loving, caring thing. Good luck with that! If their spouse does not do these things or live this way, they may think their spouse is a heathen! Narrow thinking leads people to be too critical or judgmental.

When we practice narrow thinking, we want other people to do what we think is right, or we think they are the problem. Not only are their opinions wrong, but they are wrong! They are bad, bad, bad. That is narrow thinking. The apostle Paul wrote in Philippians 2:3, "Do nothing out of selfish ambition or vain conceit, but in humility consider others better than yourselves." We are encouraged to accept the freedom in Christ. Other people have to make choices about their life, for good or for bad. Is there any area of your life where you have narrow thinking? If you are hypercritical of someone, you just might have narrow thinking.

If someone does not respond in a timely manner to a text you send or to a phone message you leave for them, do you get upset? Narrow thinking occurs when you do not allow others the freedom to respond to your texts or calls when they want to when they are able to, or how they want to respond.

If you give a gift to someone and they do not thank you for the gift or even acknowledge that they have received the gift, does that bother you? You expected some kind of grateful response. Instead, you heard nothing. Can you give them the freedom to respond in whatever way they want to respond? If that is difficult for you, you may have narrow thinking.

If you share your deepest feelings with someone and they seem to ignore what you shared, change the subject, or neglect to respond in some way to what you said, does that bother you? Will you give them the freedom to not respond to what you have said? If that is difficult for you, you may have narrow thinking.

If someone does not tell you what they are thinking or planning to do and at some point, they independently move ahead on something they obviously have decided to do, do you feel blind-sided? Do you question their motives? Do you feel slighted, controlled, or disregarded? You may have narrow thinking.

If someone does not do what you want them to do, when you want them to do it, or how you want them to do it, and that really bothers you, you might have narrow thinking. You are responsible for your own mental well-being. It is not healthy to allow your mental well-being to be dependent on what others do or do not do. You might not ever understand the reasons why people do what they do. Give them the freedom to make their own choices whether you agree with their decisions or not.

Jesus was often criticized for eating with tax collectors and sinners (Mark 2:16, Luke 15:2, Matthew 9:11). Jesus did not let this criticism bother him. Not in the least. Jesus came to seek and to save the Lost! Jesus knew early in His ministry that Judas would betray him (John 2:24-25). But Jesus gave Judas the freedom to make his own choices. Jesus' own family rejected him early in His ministry (John 7:5, Mark 3:21). Only after the resurrection did some of His family believe that He was the Son of God, the promised Messiah. Two books of the New Testament, James, and Jude, were written by the brothers of Jesus. Jesus had the long view of things. He did not have narrow thinking.

It is interesting to think about why people develop narrow thinking. Let me suggest that people tend to develop narrow thinking when they have been hurt a great deal in their life by other people. Because of this hurt, they are looking for a place where they can be free from hurt. If they can define very narrowly what is right and what is wrong, they think they are in a safe place when they can think about people and things according to their narrow viewpoint. They find their source of security in thinking that they have figured out where the right way to live is. The safe place for them is the place of their narrow thinking. Narrow thinking is a very easy thought process to fall into as a Christian. If we can define exactly where the right is and where the wrong is, then we know where the right is and where we can operate in safety. The narrow thinking person will not accept any gray areas. The amazing thing is that most people who have narrow thinking don't even realize they have narrow thinking! That is because they have justified their thinking as the right way to think and view things. They think they are right, and others who don't do what they expect are wrong. That is the sum and substance of narrow thinking.

Narrow thinking is extremely destructive in marriage. Guess what? Your spouse will not think the same about all things as you do! This is why it is important to have good communication in marriage. You have to negotiate the differences you have in marriage. It is also important to balance closeness and separateness. This is a huge issue in marriage. Ever since I was a young child, I have liked to do things with my hands. I like to build things. I like to fix things. I like to create things with my hands. The process of doing things with my hands takes time. Often, that time is separate from my wife. She respects that. I have talked to her about my need to do things with my hands numerous times. She honors my need to do things with my hands. She will allow me to work with some wood for a couple of hours, sawing, sanding, staining, gluing, nailing, etc. I need to do that. When I am doing something with my hands, I am often away from her. She will honor that time away from her if I connect with her after the time of separateness. Narrow thinking would be to say that it is wrong to want to do things with your hands and thereby to be apart from your spouse. Narrow thinking would be to say that I can rarely be with my spouse because I have a need to do something with my hands. Obviously, there has to be a balance. That balance has to be negotiated between the two people in the relationship. My wife's love language is time together and verbal sharing, so I need to spend time talking to her. We have to balance my time with my hands and her need to connect verbally and emotionally. Narrow thinking is to think it is wrong to be alone and work on things with your hands. Narrow thinking is that I should be with her all the time, being emotionally verbal with her during that time.

Let me remind you that Jesus knew perfectly how to balance His time. Jesus spent over three years with His disciples. But He took time to be alone. He had time alone on a mountain when He decided who He would call to be His disciples. He had time alone early in the morning for prayer. He had time where He spent the day with large crowds. All kinds of people felt comfortable with Jesus. The tax collectors, adulterers, and thieves felt comfortable with Jesus. Jesus did not destroy people because they did not follow God's laws perfectly. He did draw lines. He blasted the Pharisees in Matthew 23. He called them blind guides, whitewashed tombs, hypocrites. But many times, He was very patient with them. When you think about it, Jesus is the only one who really could have narrow thinking! He is the Son of God. He was involved in giving the message to the authors of the Bible so that the Scriptures could be written. He knew what was right and what was wrong. But many times, He did not use the "trump card" of His perfection. He did not call people on the carpet for what they were doing. What if God had narrow thinking with you? What would He say to you? God could confront you and me about many things. God lets a lot of things go. God knows we are all in the process of growing into new creations in Christ. Do other people feel comfortable around you? If not, you may have some narrow thinking.

A fourth destructive thought pattern is emotional thinking. Now, it is not wrong to think about our emotions and to seek to understand them. Emotional thinking is when a person feels something and then thinks it must be true because they felt it. Let me tell you, if you have not already realized it, feelings are fickle! Just because you feel something does not mean what you feel is healthy, good, or God pleasing.

Feelings are like a stream. If you are kayaking down a mountain stream, you use your weight to steer the kayak, and you use your paddles to guide you down the stream so that you do not run into rocks, trees, or other people. You navigate the rapids. You choose the best path to guide your kayak. When you go through life, it is wise to guide your thoughts by the truth of the Word of God rather than the whim of the stream of your feelings. If you do not guide your feelings down the stream of life, you will run into some rocks! You may even get capsized and thrown into the stream! You may even run into other people and possibly hurt them. We are not the hopeless slaves of our feelings. It is important that we navigate our lives through the stream of our feelings so that we end up in a good place. We want to end up in the calm waters after we get through the rapids. How are you doing at navigating your thoughts through the rapids of your feelings? How are you doing at sifting through your thoughts in each and every situation? Not always easy to do. We need God's help to do this. Again, it is not always easy to do. But God can help us. He is the guide that rides with us down the stream. He can and will help us deal with our feelings and our thoughts in a healthy way.

A man sat in my office one day. He was in tears. He had been married four times. What brought him to my office was that he could not understand how his current relationship had ended. Through tears, he said, "All I have ever wanted is to be loved." He was a believer in Christ. He went to church on a regular basis. He was a nice guy. What happened? He got in relationships with women based on the feelings of the moment, made a marriage commitment based on those feelings of the moment, and ended up feeling empty! People, both men, and women can portray a particular persona for a period of time to get what they want. The result is that people think that the person is one way when in reality they are something different. They let their emotions deceive them into believing something that is not true. Giving in to the feelings of infatuation, loneliness, or sexual attraction for the basis of a relationship usually ends up poorly. Going by the feelings of the moment is not the basis for a long-term loving relationship. Feelings can lead us astray. There is a way that seems right to a man, but in the end is death (Proverbs 14:12). In this context, a particular feeling about something may feel right, but in the end, leads to pain and suffering.

If you have strong feelings about doing something or taking some course of action, it is wise to talk with a mature, objective friend. They will not have the same feelings you have about that course of action, and they might be able to see through the smoke screen of your feelings. They may see the path to a healthier, God-pleasing life better than you do. The question is, will you talk with them about your thoughts and feelings? And will you listen to what they have to say? As you think about how you have sometimes practiced emotional thinking, how has this affected your life?

There are many examples in the Bible of people practicing emotional thinking. King David in the Old Testament had feelings for Bathsheba. Maybe he liked her bath bubbles. I think he had some feelings. I think those feelings were more from his flesh than from the Spirit of God. He thought, *At least for a moment, if I feel it, it must be real.* You can read about King David and Bathsheba in 2 Samuel 11. Emotional reasoning leads people to make decisions based on the philosophy of the old song, "How can it be wrong when it feels so right?" But making decisions based on the feelings of the moment can often lead to heartache and disobedience to God. Bathsheba may have been beautiful, but she was the wife of another man. Therefore,

Bathsheba was off-limits to David. Besides, David already had a wife. Maybe more than one. The Bible calls the desire to have another man's wife "lust." The Bible calls taking another man's wife in a physical relationship "adultery." Pretty clear. David's feelings were not right and were not God-pleasing. Be sure of this: before we take any course of action, there have been some feelings about the course of action and thoughts about that course of action. Those feelings and thoughts are the battleground of our lives. As we grow in being new creations in Christ, we grow in dealing with our feelings and our thoughts in a way that honors God.

Judas must have had some feelings that moved him to sell out Jesus for thirty pieces of silver. But look where he ended up! He ended up with so much remorse that he took his own life! We don't know exactly what Judas was feeling. But obviously, he was making a decision based on emotional reasoning. Selling out Jesus somehow made sense to him. When he realized what he had done, he tried to make it right by giving the money back to the Pharisees. They would not accept any blame in the matter. They refused to receive the repentance of Judas or the money. The result was that Judas went out from them and hanged himself (Matthew 27:3-5). Again, a decision based on emotional reasoning. How many people commit suicide because of emotional reasoning? Almost all of them. Just because you feel something does not make it true or right. It is a dangerous position to be in when we make decisions in our life on the basis of emotional reasoning.

The Apostle Peter had some feelings by the fireside when Jesus was arrested. It led to him denying he knew Jesus three times, even after he had been warned by Jesus Himself! (Matthew 26:69-75) Feelings are not the enemy. Don't play the stoic. The wrong answer to emotional reasoning would be to deny or ignore all feelings. That also is not a healthy way to live. Giving in to feelings that lead us down a wrong path is what we want to watch out for. Living life by our feelings can be a problem. It is important to separate our feelings into what is good and godly and what is wrong and not of God. We do this in our thoughts about our feelings. God can and will help us do this. If we will let Him.

Sometimes we deny our feelings or do not understand them. When this happens, we can still make decisions in our lives based on those feelings. It is important that we own our feelings and sift through them, throwing out what is not healthy and choosing what is healthy. When we deny our feelings, they are still part of who we are. Possibly even more a part of who we are because we are not dealing with them. When we deny our feelings, we ignore the impact they have on our life. Be sure of this; even if we deny our feelings exist, they are still there and will impact our decisions. They will impact our life.

This is difficult for me to share, but it has been part of my journey in life. I started this book by saying that I wanted to speak from my heart, and that is what I intend to do. My hope is that God can use what I share for good in the lives of others. I don't think I am the only one who has gone through a "dark season of the soul." This "dark season of the soul" is when you get stuck in depressive thoughts. It is when you let your negative feelings about how things are going in your life and how other people are treating you overwhelm you. I knew that this was a danger and that it was not a good thing to do. I have counseled other people who have allowed themselves to go through a "dark season of the soul." Even though I knew the right answers when it came to dealing with emotional thinking, I still let it happen to me. I let the negative aspects of my life take control of my thinking and feeling. I did not realize I was doing it at the time. Possibly you have done this too.

The amazing thing is that I really did not have a good reason to get so depressed. My marriage was doing well. We were doing fine financially. My health was good. I had friends and people who loved me. We were living comfortably. So, what was the problem? I think the problem has many facets.

One, I grew up with a self-centered, abusive father. I had hurt from my relationship with my father, even long after he had died. My father died in 2000. Sometimes I did well handling that hurt. Other times I didn't do so well. When I didn't do so well with the hurt, I struggled with the "dark season of the soul." When I ignored the hurt and pretended that it was not that important, the hurt remained and looked for a way to express itself. At times, the hurt from my father made me grieve what I did not have in my relationship with my father. At other times, the hurt from my father made me angry. That hurt made me especially angry when I thought about how he treated my mother. Hurt that is repressed will look for some relief somewhere in our lives.

Two, I coped with my pain early in life by achievement. After all, achievement was my ticket out of the abuse. I realized as a young person that if I was going to break free from the abuse my father was causing in the family, I had to become self-sufficient financially. I bought my first car at age 16 with my own money. I paid all the expenses for that car. At the end of the day, if I felt that I had worked hard and achieved my financial goals, I was doing just fine. What a lie! Being busy can be a cheap anesthetic for the pain we feel in life. It gives the illusion that we are doing fine when in reality, we are not doing well emotionally. I, therefore, thought that if I did my duties at the church the best that I could do, I was doing fine. That mindset was a form of denial. It masked my emotional pain by being busy, doing my best, going above and beyond the call of duty.

Three, I did not have the kind of childhood or adolescence that most people have. I did not have friends stay the night at my house, nor did I stay the night at any friend's house. At the time, I did not realize this was an option or something that other people were doing. I realize now that my parents did not allow this to happen, probably to make sure that other people did not know the truth about what was going on in our home. I never played organized sports as a child. I did not know when I was a child that this was an option. I realized that I was different from other young people when I played organized sports in 9th grade. I realized that the other students had been playing organized sports for a long period of time. They knew things about sports that I did not know. When I played football in 9th grade, I did not know how to put the pads on in the uniform. I realized that the other players had been playing football for a long time and that putting their pads on was something they had done numerous times for many years. I realized that I did not have that experience.

As I grew older, I realized that my childhood was different from other people my age. I realize now that if other people knew what was going on in our home, there would have been problems. There was abuse that crossed legal bounds. When there is abuse in a family, there are secrets that must be maintained lest the law finds out about the abuse and does something about the abuse. As a child, you don't realize it at the time because the abuse seems normal to you. The abuse is all that you know. I learned as a child that you just keep on going, even though you are hurting. I learned as a child to accept as normal a great deal of pain. This way of thinking is a form of denial. I did the same thing in the later years of my ministry. I thought that if you just keep going and do what you need to do, things will turn out okay. Again, another way to deny pain in my life.

Fourth, I did not receive very much teaching about life or relationships from my mother or my father. By that, I mean that neither my mother nor my father spent very much time talking to me about life, relationships, setting goals, or how to deal with feelings and process the pains of life. My father never one time in my life asked me, "How are you doing?" We did not talk about things that really mattered. My mother spent most of her energy raising four children, working as a head nurse in oncology, and dealing with my father's issues. She did not have very much left after taking care of those things. My mother was nurturing. She was very accepting. She gave me a great example of faithfulness and caring. I could go to her if I wanted to talk to her about something. The problem was that I did not go to her to talk about something unless it was really bad. She had enough to deal with. So, I realize now that I would not talk to her about what was bothering me because what was bothering me seemed trivial compared to what she was dealing with. The lesson I learned in all of this? Do not stuff your feelings. Because stuffing feelings is another form of denial.

I remember in 3rd grade, my teacher brought me in from recess early to talk with me. She must have noticed that I was struggling with something. She must have noticed that I had some issues. I can't speak for her, but she noticed something. She asked me what was bothering me. She asked me how things were going at home. I did not give her an honest answer. I was not able to share with her what was going on or how I felt. She said she would always be available to talk if, at any time, I wanted to talk. Amazingly, I still remember that incident like it was yesterday. Even today, when I drive by that school and see the playground of that school, I think of that moment. At the time, I thought that if my teacher felt that I had some problem, then I must be different from the other children in my class. I did not understand then how, but I knew there was something different about me or my life. I did not understand the abuse, nor did I know how to talk about it. What was I doing? Stuffing my feelings.

These things are not excuses. They only paint the picture that I was poorly equipped to handle emotional pain in my life. I had not seen it modeled. I was not taught by my parents how to handle emotional pain in a healthy way. Therefore, early in life, I developed certain patterns of dealing with emotional pain. These patterns would be repeated in my life, even without me realizing it.

Some of the coping mechanisms I developed worked for a while. Coping mechanisms like a good work ethic. If you work hard, you will get exhausted and will not have the time or energy to deal with your pain. Being exhausted from work can be a coping mechanism. You also get strokes from other people because you are a hard worker. Have you tried this coping mechanism? Probably you did not even realize you were using it as a coping mechanism. After all, if you are accomplishing a lot of good things, it makes you feel good about your life. The bad things don't feel all that important compared to what you have accomplished.

Another coping mechanism I used was to get my need for love and affirmation met in relationships with the opposite sex. If you can feel good in a relationship with a girl, at least for a moment, it makes the pain of life seem less severe, and it makes you feel that you can cope with your pain. I never felt it was a problem to have a relationship with a girl. I had many relationships with girls. I did things with girls that I am not proud of now. The question I have asked myself was, why? Was it conquest? Was it an attempt to deal with loneliness? Was it an attempt to feel loved? Probably all of the above. I realize now it was a way to deaden the pain I was feeling in my life. Sorry, girls. Seeking love from girls was a coping mechanism.

Some people misuse food as a coping mechanism. I did that when I was in Elementary School but overcame that as I got older. At one point in my life, I realized that I would be accepted by others, males and females, by being thin rather than overweight. Some people withdraw from others as a coping mechanism. Some people stay in bed or sleep too much as a coping mechanism. Some people get angry. Some people become manic-depressive. They go full steam ahead to accomplish more than anyone else has done until they reach the point that they crash emotionally. There are many ways that people cope with the stress and pain in their life. What is your coping mechanism?

Finally, there is the coping mechanism of drugs or alcohol. I never did drugs. I was afraid of drugs. Honestly, I have never done any drugs. I have never smoked the first marijuana joint. I did not want to do drugs and get in trouble with the law. But I did drink. In my home growing up, at least according to my father, drinking was a right-of-passage. You became a real man when you could drink. When I was a teenager, the drinking age in Florida was eighteen years old. When I turned eighteen, my father introduced me to a drink called a Stinger. A Stinger consists of two shots of brandy and one shot of Crème De Menthe. So really, one drink is three drinks. My father would smile when we would drink a Stinger together. He would not say anything. He might ask after the first Stinger, "Do you want another?" I would tell him that I did not want another Stinger. The drinking of Stingers continued for some time until I told him that I really did not like drinking Stingers. I really did not enjoy drinking straight liquor. It is interesting. A drink that is called a Stinger. A drink that not only had the name of Stinger but also a drink that could sting you. I realize now, alcohol can sting you. It can cause a wound. It can bite you. Alcohol can cause great hurt.

My parents always had a bar stocked with liquor. It seems like years ago, this was a socially acceptable thing to do. Although there was alcohol in my home growing up, I would not say my father was an alcoholic. He did not drink every day, and I never saw him drunk. I would not drink from their bar without permission. After all, I could buy whatever alcohol I wanted at the age of eighteen. For a period of time, my mother would regularly have a rum and coke when she came home from work at 3:30 p.m. Then, she would take a nap before making dinner. Drinking can be a powerful coping mechanism.

I do not want to blame anyone for my choices. I am only trying to paint a context of my life and what I was dealing with when I went through a painful "dark season of the soul" in my life.

In the later years of my ministry, things for me were very difficult. I was in the "dark season of the soul," and I would not accept that I was in the "dark season of the soul." Remember I said before, if you deny your real feelings or fail to handle them in a healthy way, they will look for a way to express themselves. Have you ever done something, then looked back on what you did and said, "What was I thinking?" Maybe, you were acting out your emotional pain without even realizing that is what you were doing. Obviously, it is much better to identify our pain, admit it to ourselves or someone else, and take steps to deal with the pain in a healthy way.

I had been at the same church for thirty years. The church was not growing. The Sunday School was declining or almost non-existent. Church attendance was stagnant. We were receiving new members. But the new members only made up for those who died or left the church. Getting people to serve in elected positions was difficult. There were many other things going on in the church that made ministry very difficult for me. My wife had been the music director at the church. She sometimes did not feel valued in her role as music director, and when she addressed some of her feelings about this to the leadership of the church, she did not feel listened to or validated. I heard about this at home. I went through it with her. I believe the way I handled that was to try to be strong for her. Being strong meant that I denied my pain. I believe that if I could provide a good example to her of how to handle the hurt that we felt, all would be just fine. My belief led me down the path of denial.

I sometimes felt hurt when I did not feel valued, listened to, or validated as the pastor of the church. I began to feel rejected as a leader of the church when my opinions seemed to be disregarded. There is a benefit in serving one church for a long period of time. You know the story of people's lives because you have lived it with them for so long. You know how they struggled in adolescence. You know what it was like for them to find a marriage partner. You have even counseled with them and their fiancé before marriage. You celebrate their marriage and the birth of their children. You are there with them when their parents age and sometimes go through illness and death. You go through life with them. That is a huge benefit.

There is also a downside of serving one church for a long period of time. People get comfortable with you. People think that since you have always been there, you will always be there. They don't feel a need to make any changes. They think that things in the church are going just fine as long as you continue to be their pastor. Listen, anything that is not changing is not growing. Growth requires change. It seemed to me during that time that any attempts I made to bring about change fell on deaf ears. It was a difficult time for me and for my wife.

When things are not really going that well at a church, some people seem to think the obvious thing, what needs to change, is the pastor. I was in a great deal of pain because of all this, but I ignored the pain. I stuffed the pain down into my innermost being. I really believed that if I just did the right thing when it came to my responsibilities, God would take care of the rest. However, I did not realize at the time how the pain was affecting me.

I found myself thinking daily about retirement. I thought to myself, *I could retire at age sixty-two. Only twenty more months. I can make it that long.* I thought about this daily. I thought about this a good part of each day. At one point, I realized that this daily thought was a way I was torturing myself. So, I decided to not think about retirement. Again, a form of denial. That worked to some degree, but it was still a difficult time. It was difficult for me to go to the office. It was difficult for me to make it through the day. I found relief when I left the office at the end of the day and did not have anything scheduled for the evening. When something did come up in the evening, a crisis phone call, or an unexpected trip to the hospital, I had to, at times, force myself to take care of the issue. Not a fun place to be.

I would not say I was burned out in ministry. Burnout happens when you work too much and do not have balance in your life. Burnout happens when you think everything depends upon you and not the Lord. I do not think I was burned out. I think I had a great deal of pain that I would not acknowledge, and I did not talk about this pain with anyone except my wife. It was a "dark season of the soul."

At one point, I told my wife, "I don't want to be a pastor anymore." This caused her great concern. I think it even scared her. I have always believed that I am capable of doing something else...teaching, being a waiter, roofing, whatever. It causes a great deal of tension to be in a position that you don't want to be in. I believe the constant thought about retirement was a way I thought I could relieve that tension. It did not relieve the tension. When I ignored the thought of retirement, I only stuffed the pain I was feeling deeper inside me.

I was not suicidal. I have never been suicidal. I was not concerned about finances. I was just depressed and would not acknowledge to myself how depressed I was. I had stuffed my feelings, hoping that they would go away. Better said, I would not admit how depressed I was to myself or to others. This is a bad place to be in. My guess is that many other church workers have been in the same place. My guess is that many other fathers and mothers, husbands and wives, even children, have been in the same place. That place is the "dark season of the soul." The only one who knew anything about this "dark season of my soul" I was going through was my wife. Bless her for hanging in there with me.

Sure, I preached at funerals, conducted weddings, contacted prospective members, cared for the sick and home-bound, preached and taught on Sunday mornings, attended meetings, answered phone calls, cared about people, counseled those in distress, but underneath it all, I knew that I was not doing well. I would not admit to myself at that time how much I was struggling to deal with everything. After all, you are the pastor. People depend on you. As a pastor, people come to you with their struggles. A pastor is supposed to have it all together. A pastor is not supposed to have problems. The pastor is close to God-at least, as close to God as anyone can be. Not true. It is amazing to me how we can portray outwardly a certain persona yet inwardly be something totally different. Yet, when you have pain that is not being resolved, that pain takes a toll. We are all only human. We all have our limits of what we can deal with. I have learned this from experience: I don't care who you are or how strong you feel you are, you can only take so much. At some point, you either get help, or you go to your coping mechanisms.

It was at that time I began to drink alcohol more heavily. I usually had a drink of wine each night before going to bed. More like four glasses of wine in a big green cup. I now know it was four glasses of wine in one cup because my wife measured it! Drinking like that was not wise, and I believe it set me up for what was going to happen next.

I was already using a coping mechanism for stress that set me up for increasing the intake of alcohol. My wife would at times challenge me about having wine each night before going to bed. I felt her challenging words about my drinking were more about her being critical of me which caused me to feel rejection and more stress and did not help me in my management of pain. I do not fault her for talking to me about my drinking. She was right to do so. Since I did not like to be challenged, I started hiding my drinking. Not good. When you are hiding your drinking from those who care about you, it is a sure sign that you have a problem.

One Christmas a few years ago, my four children, their spouses, and the grandchildren came to our home. We had a wonderful time. My oldest son and wife bought some Vodka to put in some of their mixed drinks. When they went back home, they left the remaining Vodka in the freezer in the garage. I have shared this with my son, not to blame him, but to explain what had happened. I decided to try some Vodka with some wine when I would have a drink at night. The effect was that I could feel numb quicker and not have to drink so much wine. Adding vodka to the wine was a faster way to numb the pain I was experiencing. So, I followed up on the drinking of that bottle of Vodka by buying another bottle of Vodka. And another bottle of Vodka. My wife did not know I was drinking Vodka. She could tell that something was going on because I would behave in ways that were unusual for me. I would do things that were out of character for me.

One weekend it all came to a head when my wife went away for a period of time, and I had some drinks while she was gone. When she came home, I was passed out on the couch. I was not just sleeping. I was passed out. When she woke me up, I tried to get up from the couch but passed out and fell on the floor, injuring my nose. Not a pretty picture. I do not blame anyone for this. I realize now that, at that time in my life, I was not handling my emotions very well. I was using alcohol as a coping mechanism. I own all of it.

The amazing thing is that I knew all the right answers. I knew that using alcohol as a coping mechanism was wrong. I knew what it meant to be an alcoholic. I knew it was wrong to hide my drinking. I knew it was not healthy to drink every day. I knew that I was hurting my wife and risking the respect of the people in my church who thought highly of their pastor. I knew that God was not pleased with what I was doing. What is amazing to me as I look back on it is that my wife stuck by my side. I really needed to know that she would stand by me at the time. My wife stuck by my side, but she also did something about my actions.

My wife demanded that I get some help. She called all four of our children and told them what had happened. She called her brother, also a pastor, and told him what had happened. I do not fault her for doing that. She needed a support system, and I needed to be honest. Bringing other people into the problem achieved both of those goals. She called a counselor who she had heard speak on "focus on the family" and received counsel from him. She loved me, but she drew some boundaries. She told me that she loved me but that she could not keep living like this. Something needed to change.

So, I went to a counselor. The problem is that I had a PhD in counseling, and I knew all the right answers. The counselor was not strong enough or knowledgeable enough to deal with the problem. I was too smart for that counselor, and she knew it. So, I researched Alcoholic Anonymous (AA) meetings. What is ironic is that I did my PhD thesis on the principles of the twelve steps of AA and applied them to marriage counseling. I found an AA meeting that would fit my schedule in another city. I began to go to those meetings, and I got a sponsor. A sponsor is a go-to person any time of the day or night. Someone who had been there and who had overcome the need to drink. I knew from my studies that it takes at least six months of sobriety to break the habit of drinking. I determined that I would go at least six months without drinking anything. I went to AA meetings for at least six months. I went more than six months and did not have a drink. I began the journey of facing my pain and doing something to resolve it. What also helped me during this time was that I determined a date when I would retire. Once I set that date, I knew that I would, at that time, distance myself from the stress and pain that I was dealing with. I felt a dramatic change was coming. I saw the finish line. I knew that I could make it to that finish line without using alcohol as a coping mechanism.

Pain that is not processed in a healthy way, pain that is ignored and stuffed down in your emotions, will look for some way of release. Manage your pain in a healthy way, or it will manage you. Period. Admit you are hurting. Find someone who can help you with your pain. If one person you talk with about your pain is not able to help you, find someone else. If that person is not able to help you deal with your pain, find someone else. I am glad to say that I am not a slave to alcohol today. I am glad to say I am happily married. I am glad to say that I do not have to drink to cope with life. I am glad to say I am in the process of becoming a new creation in Christ.

What pain are you feeling? What are you doing about it? Are you covering it up or dealing with it? What role is alcohol taking in your life? Is there something you need to change? Learn from others who have gone through a "dark season of the soul" before you take a fall. God already knows where you are. The good news is that God has not given up on you. God can help you. But you have to be open to His help.

We sometimes have wrong thinking about things. God wants to help us to change that. How does He do that? He has given us a manual that describes how we should think. That manual is the Word of God. He has given us an example of how to think about our lives, our future, our relationships, ourselves. His example is Jesus. Study Jesus, and you will see how He thought! Study Jesus, and you will see how He handled the pain in His life. Study the life of Jesus, and you will see how he handled difficult people. We become a new creation in Christ when we think the way Jesus thought and when we handle things the way Jesus handled things.

One last thing. There is an abundant amount of help available. The greatest source of help is the Word of God. Download the Biblical software! A computer cannot complete a particular task unless it is programmed to do that particular task. Our minds cannot think correct ways, in new ways, unless we download the right programs. The good news is that God has written the software for our thinking! God also supplies technical support by the Holy Spirit. God knows if there are any viruses in your thinking program. God can identify those faulty thinking patterns and change them. Ask yourself, or if you are brave enough, ask someone who really knows you:

1. How often do I obsess about things in my life?
2. How often do I nurse the hurts in my life?
3. In what areas of my life do I practice narrow thinking?
4. Do I tend to rely on emotions as the basis for my thoughts or the objective truth of God's Word?
5. Am I receptive to the work of God to identify destructive thinking patterns in my thoughts and to change them?
6. Do I have any destructive coping mechanisms when I feel depressed?

CHAPTER THREE

Becoming a New Creation in Your Relationships

Relationships are important. Relationships give our lives meaning. We need friends. We need to be involved with other people socially. We need to know we can count on other people to be there for us when we are going through a difficult time in our lives. We need to be there for other people who are going through a difficult time in their life. You can only do that if you have a good relationship with those people. I make it a priority to spend time talking with each of my four children. My oldest son, Matthew, makes it a point to call me or my wife on a weekly basis. Matt is not only my son, he is my friend. I have to admit, though, he reaches out to me more than I reach out to him! I really appreciate that about him. I enjoy talking with all my children. It is interesting that as you get older, your children become your friends, not just your children. I enjoy being with each one of them. The point is, it is important if you want to have a relationship with someone that you are intentional about connecting with that person. You need to make a choice to reach out to someone. If you simply only reach out when the need arises, the relationship will suffer.

One of the benefits of being involved in a local church is that we do life together with other people. We worship together and serve together. Because of our involvement in a church, we have built into our lifetimes for connection. The times for connection involve weekly worship, Bible studies, serving together in some way. In the church, we can celebrate life with one another. We can grieve with one another. We can grow in our faith together. The church is a wonderful place to grow in relationships with other people. Of course, there are sports clubs, community groups, other service groups, but none of them offers such a close personal connection in relationships like the church.

When a baby is born in a family, everyone celebrates in the church! When young people reach some kind of achievement, everyone celebrates! When people get married, and many church members are invited because there is already an established connection, everyone celebrates! In a similar way, when one family experiences hardship or loss, everyone grieves with them. I remember one man who suffered from a stroke. He was limited in what he could speak as well as what he could do. His wife died suddenly. His wife was his primary caretaker. When I visited him in his home, I asked him how he was doing. He was sitting on the couch in his TV room. There was a large box on the coffee table in front of him. The box was filled with hundreds of sympathy cards from members of the church. He answered my question by holding up the box and excitedly saying that he was not alone. He said, "Look at all the people that care about me and that are praying for me!" That, my friends, is one of the benefits of having good relationships with people in a church. You will never be alone. At least, that is the way Christ wants the church to work.

In our day, many people are starving for relationships with others. Because of the pandemic, we have lockdowns and social distancing. We wear masks that cover our faces. For a while, churches were closed down. The church services were virtual, consisting of a few musicians and the pastor. Even as I write this, most churches are limiting how many people can come to church. Some churches control the number of people who can come to church by requiring people to sign up for church each Sunday. Because of the pandemic, relationships are struggling in the church. This is a tough time for churches in our country. When people are fearful of the virus so that they do not go to church, they cannot really connect with others. Some people stay home because they do not want to risk getting infected. The effect of all this? It leads to loneliness.

It is also a tough time for families. Grandparents cannot spend time with their grandchildren because there is the fear that the grandparents may contract a virus from the grandchildren or that the grandchildren will contract the virus from the grandparents. Some grown children have even banned their parents from spending time with their children. Sure, you can talk on the phone or FaceTime, but it is not the same as person-to-person contact.

Some people have reduced their interaction with other people to some form of social media platform. Connecting with people through social media is not as effective as a face-to-face encounter. Connection through social media is easier and quicker, but it is also more sterile than face-to-face connection. In face-to-face connection, you can look someone in the eyes, you can hear the inflection in their voice, you can feel their body language, you can have meaningful touch. Social media robs you of a good part of that kind of connection.

God cares about our relationships. Do you notice a theme in this book? God cares about how we live in every aspect of our lives because He wants us to maximize the time we have on earth. One way we maximize our time on earth is to have good relationships with others. God wants us to be the best we can be in Christ, to be new creations. Therefore, God cares about our relationships.

In the very beginning, God said to Adam, "It is not good for the man to be alone!" (Genesis 2:18) We need relationships, but we need good, healthy relationships. When Jesus was asked what the greatest commandment was, He said the greatest commandment was to love the Lord with all your heart, soul, mind, and strength. Then He said the second greatest commandment is to love your neighbor as yourself. And who is our neighbor? Read Luke 10, and you will find out what Jesus thinks. Our neighbor is not just the people who live next door to us. Our neighbor is not only our family members. Our neighbor is anyone who is in need, and let me tell you, everyone has needs! God definitely is interested in our relationships. How do we become new creations in Christ in our relationships?

If we really want to have good relationships, it is vital that we overcome our fears. This is ironic. One of our greatest fears is to feel unloved. When we give in to the fear that we might not be loved by someone, we actually block the flow of love in our life. If we have fear in our relationships, we will allow distance between us and others so that we can protect ourselves from pain or rejection.

One time I had a counseling session with a beautiful young girl. She was at that time in high school. In the course of our conversation, I asked her, "What is your greatest fear?" She said what she feared the most was not being loved by others. Did she mean she wanted a boyfriend? No, that was not what she feared. She could have had a boyfriend at any time if she wanted one. Did she mean she did not feel accepted by her peers, that she was a loner? No, I knew better than that. She was active in different school groups and in the youth ministry of our church. Did she mean she did not feel loved by her parents? No, they had done all they could do to show her their love. What she wanted was to feel that no matter what she did, she would be accepted for who she was. What she wanted was to know that she was important to someone, that she was special to someone, that she was valued. What blocked her from getting that need met was the fear that people would not accept her as she was, value her for who she was, love her just as she was.

Here is the key to dealing with our fear of not being loved by others. Other people cannot meet our deepest need for relationship. Only God can. Once you know that you are loved unconditionally by God, you can overcome the fear of not being loved. You already know that you are loved! By God, nonetheless! When you know you are loved by God, it helps you overcome the fear of being rejected by others. Will you get rejected by others? Absolutely! Will it take time to process that rejection in your thinking and emotions? Absolutely. But you can overcome the rejection when you know God loves you. Doubt that you are loved by God? Look at the cross. God so loved you that He gave His one and only Son for you (John 3:16). That is the greatest love anyone has ever seen or experienced. There is no fear in love, that is, in God's perfect love (1 John 4:18). Do not live your life with the fear that you will not be loved by others. God has already shown you that He loves you no matter what you do.

Another way to become new creations in Christ in our relationships is to resolve relationship breakdowns. Relationship breakdowns occur when there is unresolved hurt in our relationships. Relationship breakdowns occur when people do not talk with one another or avoid one another. Relationship breakdowns occur when people are not willing to forgive one another. People feel great pain in their lives when important relationships break down. Sometimes a husband and wife may have a relationship break down and end up feeling like they are two strangers living in the same house. Sometimes there is a relationship breakdown between a parent and a child so that they do not see one another or talk with one another. Sometimes there are relationship breakdowns between siblings. These broken relationships can be restored. There is a Biblical way to do that.

God sent His Son to be our Savior so that the relationship breakdowns between us and Him could be reconciled. God wants to help us resolve relationship breakdowns in our relationships with others. The word reconcile means to make two people who are at odds with one another into one. Something divided you, be it hurt, misunderstanding, or a power struggle. When you reconcile, you find a way to become one again. You tear down the dividing wall between you. Both people must be involved in this process, or the reconciliation will not occur. One of the greatest ways to reconcile a relationship is through confession and absolution. Whenever there is a relationship breakdown, there has been some kind of sin that has impacted the relationship. Often, we want to pin the sin problem on the other person, thereby justifying ourselves. This creates an "I am right, and you are wrong" dynamic. This means you want to be right in what you have done, and the other person is wrong. The result is that you are the winner, and the other person is the loser. How does that work for relationships? Not very well. What you want in your relationships is a win-win situation. That can only be achieved when each person owns their responsibility in the relationship breakdown and takes steps to reconcile the relationship.

When I counsel married couples, I ask each partner to come in for a session with me by themselves. I have found out that each married person will talk more openly with me when they are not in the presence of their partner. I simply ask them, "So, what is going on? What do you think the problems are in your relationship, and what have you done to try to resolve them?" Then I get silent. I want to listen. I want them to open up to me, to spill their heart out. I usually write down what they say to me so that I can remember what was said, pray about it later, and study what was said for certain patterns and inconsistencies. I do this with just about every couple I counsel about their marriage. After meeting with each of them separately, I meet with the couple together. I share with them from their own testimony, ways they have been hurtful to one another, and their relationship. Then I give them some homework. I ask them to write down how they have been hurtful to their spouse and to their relationship. These hurts can be in thought, word or deed. I ask them to write this down so that they can share it during the next counseling session. They are to finish the sentence, "When I did this, said this, thought this, I was hurtful to you and to our relationship, and I am sorry for that." After one partner shares what they have written, I ask the other partner if they are willing to forgive them? We practice confession and absolution. Confession and absolution is a very powerful process. When your partner confesses their wrongs to you, it builds your trust in your partner when you see that they are willing to own what they have done that has been hurtful. It also builds good will in your own heart when you hear your partner forgive you. I have seen couples do this in a counseling appointment, and by the end of the session, both of them are crying. There is a release of the hurt. There is reconciliation.

There is a local city magazine that is published in our community and mailed free of charge to every household in our town. One of the articles in the magazine is an article by a local pastor. I have been asked several times to contribute an article to the magazine. One of the articles I submitted was on marriage. Let me tell you, it is tough for a pastor to address a topic in 150 words or less! Here is the article that I submitted in the May 2018 edition of the magazine:

Dr. Russell Frahm,

Marriage is a special gift from God. Too often though married people are merely existing together. The fire of their love has died down. The sparks don't fly much anymore. Their emotional intimacy and their physical intimacy is, well, smoldering. Okay, enough fire analogies! The truth is, with God's help, you can fan the flames of love, kindle romance and get really stoked about one another!

Have fun together. It is easier to love someone when they are fun to be around. Business is a sun killer. It is vital to balance the competing demands in your life so you can make marriage-building a priority. Do some of the craze things you did together when you were dating. Remember how good it feels to hold your spouse's hand on a walk around the block? Go on a picnic in a park. Find a secluded beach and hang out. Laugh a lot. Love rest on trust, honesty, and plain old fun. It is only when those foundations are built and maintained that oneness, the self-giving union of two souls, is possible.

When was the last time you and your spouse had FUN? When was the last time you laughed together? When was the last time you stopped hurrying around enough to have a good conversation? When was the last time you really made love? Schedule time to give undivided attention to one another. Put it on the calendar! Turn off the TV. Silence the phones. Talk and touch and treasure and team up with one another.

Marriage is not about finding the right person. It is about being the right person. It is not about getting. It is about giving. The word in Genesis for a man and a woman being "united" means "to glue." A literal translation would be: "to meld two separate entities together to form a permanent bond." This is the way marriage was intended to work. God designed marriage to be a life-long union. It need not be a prison sentence. Married love can grow and glow, just like a fire. Why not turn the heap up!

An amazing thing happened when the article was published. A medical doctor in another city got a copy of the magazine and read the article. He called me and asked for an appointment for him and his wife. We practiced the homework of confession and absolution. We had a session where the couple practiced confession and absolution. It was amazing. The hurt that had built up over the years melted away like butter on a hot summer day. Good things in their relationship began to happen. Where there had been walls of division, there was now understanding and caring. What made the difference? Confession and absolution. Grace upon grace.

All of us mess up in our relationships. The level of the hurt in our relationships will determine the level of our intimacy. If there is a great deal of hurt, the intimacy will diminish. If the hurt level is low, there will be an open door for intimacy.

Another way to become new creations in Christ is to connect on a deeper level with others. Soul mates have that connection. You can be a soul mate with your wife or husband if you are married. My wife and I were watching a rerun of the 90's TV show "Home Improvement" starring Tim Allen. Tim and his wife Jill were dealing with the question, "What is a soul mate?" Tim went to the fence. If you have seen the show, you know that Tim often counsels with his neighbor, Wilson, over the backyard fence. Wilson is not really a counselor, but he functions in that role in every episode! How is it that Wilson is in his backyard every time someone wants to talk? My guess is that he spends a great deal of time in his backyard, maybe so he can find out what is going on next door! Wilson seems to be always available when there is a problem that Tim or Jill need to talk about. Wilson is almost as available as God. God is available all the time! In that episode of the show, Tim asked Wilson how one can become soul mates with one's spouse. Wilson told Tim that when you are soul mates, you want to do things your partner wants to do even if you don't want to do them. So, Tim surmised that if Jill wants to go to the opera, he should go to the opera. That did not sit right with him. If your partner wants to go to a book club, you go with them. You get the idea. After we watched that episode, I said to my wife that we were soul mates.

I explained that the "soul" (sole) is the bottom of your shoe. If you go to the same places with your partner, the "soul" of your shoe is going to the same place as the "soul" of your partner's shoe. Therefore, you are "soul" mates! I reminded her that we had been to Europe a few times, to Ethiopia and to Jamaica. So, since we had been to many places together, we must be "soul" mates. She said, and I quote, "You are so clever." I think that was a compliment. Soul mates in marriage connect with one another in meaningful ways, positive ways, in the kitchen, traveling, working, in the bedroom. More about that last one later! Good marriage relationships take work. They don't happen by accident. Good relationships with others require a lot of work. If you neglect any relationship, guess what happens? Emotional distance creeps in. It is like a slow leak in your roof. You may not see the visible results at first, but be assured, mold is growing in the attic! If you neglect the leak, the mold will become visible and affect your health! In marriage, if you neglect connection problems in your relationship, you will begin to feel like two people living in the same house. You will begin to feel that you love your partner, but you are not in love with them. It can also happen in our relationships with friends. If you neglect a relationship with a friend, emotional distance will creep into the relationship. You may care about a friend, but if you no longer connect with them, emotional distance will creep into your relationship. Don't let that happen.

You can also be a "soul mate" with other people. How do you do that? You connect with one another. You connect your hearts. Intimacy has been defined as "in-to-me-you-see." The depth of your relationship with anyone is directly related to the depth of your sharing. I tell people in counseling that you cannot love someone that you do not understand, and you cannot understand someone if they will not share themselves with you. I know most men are lousy at sharing their feelings. I have even had some men say they cannot share emotionally with their wives. The truth is, it is not that they cannot share emotionally, but rather, they will not. All of us have feelings. Sharing our feelings is a way we can connect with others. Feelings can be shared. It will require a price to be paid. You have to work on understanding how you feel and how you can frame your feelings into words. More about this in the chapter on being a new creation verbally.

Connection in relationships happens when we give one another time, trust, and talking.

Giving someone your time says to them that you value your relationship, and you are willing to arrange things in your life so that you can spend time with them. When you do not have time for someone, you are saying to them by your actions that you really do not care about the relationship you have with them. Jesus did what? He chose twelve men to be His disciples. He said to them, "Follow me." When they did follow Him, they gave up their occupations, their family, to some degree, and other friendships, to be with Jesus. They walked with Jesus. Might I add "a lot!" They ate with Jesus. They slept with Jesus. They listened to Jesus. They gave time to the relationship, and Jesus gave time to them. Do you have time for others? Jesus did. If we want to be like Jesus, we will grow in this aspect of our lives.

You give time to someone when you give them focused attention. If I am talking with someone and I keep looking at my watch or look away to others for a way of escape or point my feet and my body in another direction, I am not giving this person my focused attention. In effect, we are saying by our body language, "Time is up!" That is one of the signals I sometimes give my wife when I am ready to go somewhere or I am ready to take a break in a discussion. I am saying by my body language that I do not have time for her. I have done this, and so have you!

If a neighbor comes over to my house when I am outside working on the car and they begin to ask all kinds of questions, what do I do? I have to admit I am not always very good at this. I have sent them subtle hints that I don't have time for them, that they are interrupting me. The question I should ask myself is: is my relationship with my neighbor important? The answer? If my relationship with my neighbor is important to God, then it is important to me. Besides, many times it is when you are talking with a neighbor about cars or the weather that the really important stuff starts to come up. You have to be willing to do the chit-chat in order to take the relationship to a deeper level. And that takes time.

It is also important to budget your time. Sure, there are things that come up in the spur of the moment. Some of these things are a priority, and we must give time to them. There are also things that can take place if we intentionally set aside time for them. Be sure of this, "stuff" will take up the time that is available to them. Stuff like the TV, entertainment, whatever. Budget your time. Set aside an evening to be with someone. When you go to lunch with someone, give them your time. Turn off your phone and put it down. If you are doing something with someone on a Saturday, let's say you budget your time and tell them, "I would really like to be with you. I can do that in the morning, say from 9 am until noon. Then I have some other things I need to do." Is that cold? Not at all. It is wise. I can't tell you how many times I have seen married people get into power struggles over their use of time. She wants him to give her an evening of focused attention. He is willing to give that to her on Saturday morning, but not on the evening she wants his attention. She wants his unfocused attention, but he wants to do something else. What happens is that he feels controlled and does not give her focused time, so she gets hurt. When Saturday comes around, they are still recovering from the misdirected evening. He does not want to feel controlled, and she does not want to feel hurt by his lack of attention. They may spend much of their Saturday working through those feelings. Hopefully, they do work them through by talking about them and negotiating some way to make a change in how they manage their time. How much better for him to say, "I can sense that you want to do something together. We have from 6 p.m. until 10 p.m. available to us tonight. What if I do this particular thing, say from six to eight p.m., and then we do something together from eight to ten?" Most women will say to their husbands that you can do your thing from six to seven p.m., and then you are mine! Just kidding. Most women will agree to the six to eight and eight to ten arrangement if they trust that their partner will really be focused on them during the agreed upon time. Budget your time.

I do this with my wife when we go shopping together. I am not a good shopper. I confess with shame that I am shopping-challenged. Was Jesus a good shopper? I think not! He did not go shopping! He could just turn a few crackers into a bunch of loaves of bread! No shopping required! Besides, there were no malls or grocery stores back then! But, if need be, Jesus could be a wonderful shopping partner. So can we. What I say to my wife when we are going shopping together is, "Let's get some agreement on how long we will be shopping." If I agree to an hour, I will be the best co-shopper there could be. Well, maybe not as good as her girlfriends, but the best shopper I can be. If I think we are going shopping for a half hour and she thinks the shopping-bonding experience is going to be three hours, you can see that this misunderstanding can lead to tension or conflict. It does not need to turn out like this. Control your time, or it will control you. Budget your time. Negotiate your time with your partner if you are married. Prioritize what you want to do so that you don't waste time doing what is not very important and end up neglecting what is really important. Establish your priorities and budget your time to reflect your priorities.

As a pastor, my time had to be guarded. I could not cash in what was best for what was good. It is good to chit-chat with people that stopped by the office from time to time. Some days a lot of people stopped by the office! But if I spent a great deal of time chit-chatting, I would not have the time to pray, study, listen to the Lord, work on a message, do planning, and other important tasks that impact the congregation. If I let time get away from me, I would not be able to do the things that I really needed to do because I simply would not have the time to do them. I needed time to study and to pray about a message I was working on. Sometimes a message would take very little time. Thank God for that! Sometimes a message would take a great deal of time. I had to budget my time so that I could do what was most important.

Take dealing with salespeople as an example. Rarely would a salesperson be able to get into my office. I had charged my secretary with the task of screening the salespeople. Often the product a salesperson wanted to sell was not even my decision to make! As an example, copier salespeople would come in our church office on a regular basis. I did not want to have anything to do with buying, leasing or upgrading copiers. It was not my decision to make. I gave that decision to someone else. I would not meet with copier salespersons.

Once in a while, I would talk with one of the other salespeople that would stop by. Usually, they would get access to me when one of them would say, "I am Steve, and I would like to talk with Pastor Frahm." When a salesperson would get entry into my office, I would seek to budget my time. I know that they will want to chit-chat for a while. You know chit-chat involves questions like: How do you like the weather? How are things going at the church? Etc. Chit-chat takes time. I know that they will want to pitch their product, to try and get me to believe in their product as much as they do. That takes time. I know they will want to walk me down Decision Road. They will want to see what level of commitment I will land on, kind of like a board game. Then they will want to satisfy any objections that would keep me from moving to another space on the board of commitment. That takes time. Then they will want to close the deal. That takes time. What if I do not want to give my time to the sales process? I have to budget my time. So, I have said to salespersons, "I will give you three minutes. Make the best pitch you can. Leave some information with me, and if I am interested, I will get back to you." Sounds harsh? Not really. I have to budget my time, and so do you.

Another ingredient for good relationships is to have high trust. That means you are real, honest, and authentic with one another. In high trust relationships, the shields of protection have to come down. When it comes to matters of our heart, there is an open-door policy in our relationships. It has been said that a friend knows all about you and loves you just the same. Friends trust that you have their best interests at heart. Friends trust that they can tell you anything, and you will not use the information to injure them. Friends trust that you will accept them even if you disagree with them. Friends trust that you will be honest with them about what you will do and what you will not do in the relationship. You will not play games with them. You will not say one thing and do another thing. High trust is vital to good relationships.

If I learn that a person has not told me the whole truth and nothing but the truth, trust in the relationship is diminished. If I learn that someone has talked about something that I shared with them in confidence with others, trust in the relationship is diminished. If I find that someone had worked relationships toward some goal to accomplish what they wanted to see happen, and they have not included me in the process, trust in the relationship is diminished. If I find that someone has been hiding something from me, trust is diminished. If someone does not give me clear answers to my questions, trust in the relationship is diminished. If someone does not answer my phone calls or texts, trust in the relationship is diminished. If someone is warm and inviting one day and cold and aloof the next day, trust in the relationship diminishes. We have all seen these hurtful relationship practices happen in our relationships. We have all done these types of things in our relationships with others. Maintaining trust in our relationships requires a great deal of work. How are you doing at keeping the trust level strong in your relationships? How are you dealing with the trust relationship bombs that happen in your relationships? Trust me, strong trust in relationships take constant, conscious effort. It will not happen by chance. Trust in relationships only happens when we make that kind of trust an important relationship value in our lives. How important is high trust to you in your relationships?

Finally, good relationships are built by talking. My children call it "hanging out." In the process of hanging out, people can talk about whatever they want, whatever comes to their mind, and they believe that what they say will not be judged. Call it a "No-judge Zone." When you are sitting with people around a campfire, what happens? Smores! Well, that may be true, but the people sitting around the campfire shoot the breeze. They talk openly and connect. When you are fishing (notice I said fishing, not catching), the same thing happens. What do people do when they are fishing? They talk! During a pole-holding session, there can be a lot of talking. What did Jesus do during all those hours of walking from town to town? He talked with His disciples. Relationships are built stronger when there is time to connect when there is high trust and lots of talking.

Women generally like to talk. Men generally like silence. Silence is safe. When my wife and I are on a long road trip, and there is a long period of silence, I know she will eventually ask one particular question. She will ask, "What are you thinking?" That is a bid for connection. I might say that I am thinking about the weather or politics. Probably not true. I sometimes say I am thinking about many things all at the same time.

Or I might say that I have been thinking about something in the past that I feel I have not fully made peace with. I know my wife wants to talk. And that is okay. How good are you at talking when there are periods of silence? How good are you at answering someone who gives you a bid for connection? How much time do you spend in silence, and how much time do you spend talking about your feelings and thoughts? What would be the percentage of time you spend talking? When there is a family get-together, do you sit on the couch and watch how things are going? Or do you engage with others? Do you work on finding things to talk about with others in order to connect with them? Some people have no problem talking. Some people talk too much and do not leave room for others to talk. Most people do not talk. They prefer silence. They prefer to play it safe. They only talk when asked a question. They talk only when they feel they need to talk. What kind of person are you? How do you deal with someone who does not talk very much? How do you feel about your relationship when someone rarely talks with you? Some people talk too much. They wear people out with their many words. Usually, someone who talks too much is not a good listener. Usually, they manipulate the conversation so that they feel secure in the discussion. Be honest, are you a person who feels uneasy with silence? Do you tend to talk too much? Both extremes, not talking very much at all, or talking too much, can be hurtful to relationships. How are you doing at being a new creation in Christ when it comes to your relationships?

Here are some easy intimacy-level evaluation questions. How would you answer them?

1. What is your greatest joy today or in the last week?
2. When do you feel the most at peace?
3. What is your greatest struggle today or in the last week?
4. Do you have any relationship breakdowns that need to be resolved?
5. Do you budget your time so that you can give time to what is really important?
6. Do you have high trust in your relationships? How do you accomplish that?
7. Do you openly share what you are feeling and who you are with others?

When you ask someone questions like this, you are giving other people a bid for connection. You are saying, "Hey, I want to connect with you on a deeper level. I want to grow closer to you. Help me understand what is going on with you inside your heart." If they answer you and you listen to what they are saying, you will grow in your relationship. If you share these kinds of things with others, you will grow into a new creation in Christ in your relationships.

CHAPTER FOUR

Becoming a New Creation Physically

Our physical well-being is very important. Just as a four-cylinder car motor cannot function very well if one of the cylinders is not working well, we as people cannot function very well if our physical well-being is not working well for us. I have a huge amount of emotion as I write this chapter because I am reflecting back on people that I have known who have struggled with their physical well-being. I know people today that silently weep because they have not taken care of their physical appearance. I know people who silently weep because of their physical limitations. They have physical limitations because they have not taken good care of their physical well-being. I love them. I weep with them and for them. I would like to change them. But I can't do that. Only they can change their physical well-being by the power of God. I can help them. But I cannot change them.

Physical well-being is a huge area of life for me. Why is our physical well-being such an important area of our life? I have seen young people who are so overweight that they cannot, really cannot, go on outings with groups or with family members because they have not taken control of their physical well-being. They are physically unable. I have seen people suffer from cancer, diabetes, respiratory problems, and other debilitating conditions because they have not taken care of their physical well-being. I have seen older people simply give up on life. I have seen them sit in a chair, watch TV, do little activity, waste away physically and mentally because they have not taken steps to take care of their well-being. I have seen people feel rejected by others in society because of their lack of attention to their physical appearance. I have experienced the emotional pain of being looked down upon by others because of my physical appearance. As a young person, I was extremely overweight. I could not do the physical things that other people my age could do. It hurts me deeply to see people struggle in life because of their poor physical well-being choices. How you perceive your physical appearance and how well you are physically has a great deal to do with how well you are living your life. It has a great deal to do with how effective you are in living as a new creation in Christ. Our physical well-being has a lot to do with the quality of our lives.

It hurts me deeply to see people struggle with self-esteem issues because they do not like how their bodies look or how others treat them because of their physical appearance. I grieve when a beautiful young girl does not look me in the eye because she is ashamed of her body. I am grieved when a young man thinks he is a nobody because he does not look like a bodybuilder. I am grieved when people make choices that compromise their health and wreck their futures because they have cashed in the pleasure of the moment on some kind of drug. I grieve when I see a young girl cut herself. I grieve when I see a young man be so messed up on drugs that he cannot even carry on a conversation. I grieve when I see young girls think that love can be found in the back seat of a car. I grieve when I see people at any age give up on their physical well-being. I grieve deeply about that. I grieve because it does not have to be that way. Physical appearance and physical well-being can change for the better. Physical well-being can improve through time. The body changes, our countenance changes, as we become new creations in Christ. This is hard work. But it can be done. It can be done by the power of God. When it comes to physical well-being, never, never, never, ever give up. Never.

Each person is created with three areas of being: body, soul, and spirit. All three are related. In other words, what happens in the body will affect the soul and spirit. If you do not feel well physically, it can affect your thinking and your relationship with God. If you have some physical pain, you may give in to the pain and forfeit physical activity rather than work through the pain. You may think, "Exercise causes pain; therefore, I will not exercise!" You may begin to think your physical limitations are normal and accept them as just a part of your life. You may begin to think that because you do not feel well physically that God has somehow abandoned you. Our current physical condition needs not to control our thinking, our relationship with God, or our physical well-being. The reality is, God has not abandoned you! God wants to be involved in your well-being choices. God may want you to make some changes in your physical well-being so that you feel better. Those changes are part of what it means to become a new creation in Christ.

What happens in the soul or in your thinking can affect the body and the spirit. If you are not thinking in a healthy way, those thoughts can affect how you feel physically and also affect your relationship with God. Our bodies can only respond to what happens in our brain. If we think negative thoughts, our bodies will agree with the negative thoughts and start to manifest what corresponds to our negative thinking. If you think that you will have a stressful day dealing with your children, your spouse, or with the cares of life, your body will start to respond to that thinking by either wanting to flee, to get away, or to retreat. You may want to respond to the stress by lashing out at others or overreacting to the situation. In your thinking, trust that God knows what you will face each day and that God has the resources to help you deal with the stress of each day. Trust that with the help of God, you will do just fine. Don't let stress cause you all kinds of anxiety! Trust that God has built wonderful healing properties into your body and that through time, God can help you overcome physical pain. Your thinking can affect your physical well-being. You can think that you are going to have a no-good, rotten day, and guess what? That is what you will have!

What happens in the spirit will affect the body and the soul. If you are not giving attention to your spirit and to your relationship with God, you may not think correctly about your life or feel strong physically. The control center of our lives is our spirit, our relationship with God. Once that relationship is strong, our thinking will be changed for the better, and our bodies will respond much better. So, it is very important that we become good stewards of our body, of our physical well-being. It is very important that we give attention to our body, soul, and spirit. In this chapter, we will focus on our physical well-being. Our physical well-being can help us become new creations in Christ.

Do you believe that with God's help, you can change your physical well-being and your physical appearance? I hope you do! Because with the help of God, you can!

Often, as people age, they let their physical well-being and their appearance go to pot! They may even develop a pot belly! They develop all kinds of physical problems. Then they begin taking all kinds of medications to deal with their poor physical well-being choices. Often this simply masks the real problem. The real problem is that they have not been very good stewards of their physical well-being during their life. It is not wrong or sinful to take medications. Medications have their role in our well-being. I am sixty-four years old and do not take any medications. I very rarely take ibuprofen or aspirin. I admit, though, I have not always done what is best for my physical well-being. Very few people do. None of us is perfect! But I believe with a few lifestyle changes, we can all be healthier physically. You may even be able to reduce the medications you are taking, or you may be able to eliminate them altogether. I am not a medical doctor. I am not telling you what to do about your medications. I am saying that there may be a better way to be more healthy and not take as many medications.

When I went to my 40th high school reunion, I was surprised at what I saw. It was rather obvious who took care of their physical well-being and who did not. Athletic guys who had been in top shape in high school, now forty years later, were woefully out of shape. Besides their lack of hair, some of the guys had seen their waist size double since high school! Some of the girls I knew in high school, I did not even recognize at the reunion because they looked nothing like they did in high school. Can you believe it?

Before you start to judge me for being too critical, let me admit that I don't look like I did when I graduated from high school either! I have gained twenty pounds since high school. Twenty pounds! That would be a weight gain of about half a pound per year on average. Since I lift weights on a regular basis, I attribute the weight gain to the additional muscle! Just kidding. My wife says that when she met me at age twenty-three, I was really "buff." Whatever that means. We all age, and our bodies change through time. I have noticed as I age that some things don't work like they used to, while some things do stuff that they never did before. Like growing hair on the top of your ears. The hair may as well grow on the top of your ears because it is not growing as it used to on the top of my head!

How many people have fallen for the sales pitch to buy something that will give them a total body makeover? Have you? I have. Some years ago, we bought a home ab machine. If I could have abs like the people in the sales brochures, then this purchase would be well worth the money! We bought the ab machine. We put it on our back porch. We used it for a couple of weeks. We decided it was not fun to use, nor would it make much of a difference in our abs. That machine ended up on the curb for the garbage collector. Have you ever bought a treadmill or stationary bicycle only to use it a few times, and then it becomes something to hang your clothes on? Have you ever bought a gym membership only to say to yourself a few months later, what was I thinking? Have you bought new exercise clothes thinking that the clothes would make a difference in your commitment to exercise? Well, they did for a few times, but not in the long haul. How do we become new creations in Christ physically? I will write in this chapter about five areas of well-being. Evaluate how you are doing in each area. Be honest. The only one you will fool is yourself. If you want to become new creations in Christ physically, it involves little changes done consistently over a long period of time. There are no shortcuts. Sorry.

Exercise: Here are two insights that can help you when it comes to exercise. One, do some kind of physical activity on a regular basis. It could be walking, bicycling, jogging, tennis, yoga, whatever. The key is to do it on a regular basis. I tell myself when I don't feel like exercising, "Just get started, and God will carry you through!" Just get to the gym, and God will take over! That works most of the time. My wife has been a good inspiration for my exercise routine, especially since our gym closed recently due to the coronavirus. She has found all kinds of things for us to do for exercise via the internet. There is internet yoga. There are internet pool noodle workouts. There are thirty-minute weightlifting programs on the internet. I may not have enjoyed all of them, but the point was to do something. My wife and I sometimes go for walks after our devotions, and we pray as we walk. I wonder what our neighbors think about two older people walking down the street talking out loud to God? We have a path now in the street that we have worn by walking and praying at 6 a.m.! The point is to do some kind of physical activity on a regular basis. Don't tell me you are too busy. We find the time to do what is important to us. Can you make time to do some physical activity for thirty minutes each day? Sure you can. If you want to.

The second insight is to do something that you enjoy. If you do not enjoy what you are doing, you will probably not keep doing it! That is why we vary our exercise routine regularly. I may not feel like walking today or doing some workout program on the internet, but I can go for a bicycle ride! But I do not want to go for a bicycle ride every day. Good for you if you like to do that. I don't. But I will do it about once a week. Especially in the morning when it is cooler, and there is less traffic! I can tell you that after a ten-mile bike ride, I am done riding bikes for a while! The point is to do something every day for a short period of time and vary your exercise. It will keep you going.

People want big changes instantly. Staying fit does not work that way. You can become a new you by doing something, however small, consistently, over time. How do you move a mountain? One shovel at a time. How do you walk a mile? One step at a time. How do you lose weight? Hate to say it, one ounce at a time. As the slogan goes for one clothing apparel business: just do it! Don't tell me that you don't have the time to do some physical activity. The truth is–you have time to do whatever is important to you. If it is important to you to do some regular exercise, you will find the time to do it. For me, it works a lot better to exercise in the morning. I tell people at the gym, "I get here early before I fully wake up and realize what I am doing!" Just do a half-hour a day. You can do it! I promise you that if you exercise early in the morning, it will get your blood moving, your mind activated, your metabolism kick-started, and will positively affect your sense of well-being the rest of your day.

Diet: Another aspect of being a new creation in Christ is to watch your diet. It has been said that you are what you eat. It can also be said that you are how much you eat! I used to watch my father eat a whole block of cheese at night watching TV. It can be done. I witnessed it! No wonder his cholesterol was off the charts! If you eat ice cream every night, don't be surprised if your waistline gradually expands. If you eat out at restaurants on a regular basis, don't be surprised if you gain weight. For one, when you eat out at a restaurant, you don't expend energy to buy, cook and clean up after you eat at home! You also don't have any control over how the restaurant prepares the food. A little secret: The restaurants don't prepare the food so that you can be healthy and thin. They prepare the food so that it tastes good, and you will come back! Besides, think about all the money you spend eating out. What if some of that eating out money could be used for the sake of the kingdom of God or the good of others? What if some of that money could be used for a gym membership? Just think. I am not opposed to eating out. I love the bread and olive oil at Carrabba's! But it would not be wise to eat there all the time. All things are lawful for me or permissible, but I will not be mastered by any of them! (1 Corinthians 10:23)

I do not want this to be another diet book. There are enough of those. There is the Atkins Diet, the Whole 30 diet, the Dukan Diet, the Dubrow Diet, DASH Diet, Keto Diet, Body Type Diet, Bulletproof Diet, Cabbage Soup Diet, Apple Cider Vinegar Diet, Vegan Diet, Pegan Diet, Macrobiotic Diet, Alkaline Diet, Amish Diet (That sounds spiritual?), Daniel Fast, TB12 Method (Tom Brady Diet), Gluten-free Diet, 20/20 Diet (Dr. Phil Diet), TLC Diet, Vertical Diet, Hormone Diet, Lectin-free Diet, Grapefruit Diet, and more. Need I go on? That being said, in the Bible, our diet is important!

Why did Daniel in the Old Testament want only a specific diet? He did it not only for spiritual reasons but also for physical reasons. He believed he would be healthier if he had a specific diet. Now I am not advocating a vegetarian diet. I like eating meat, and I will probably eat some kind of meat almost every day until I die! I guess that would mean I am not a vegetarian! I am only making the point that we are what we eat. Why did God specify all the dietary laws in the Book of Leviticus? You can read about those dietary laws in Leviticus 11 and 17. In the New Testament era, we are not bound by these dietary laws. I only mention them to make the point that in the Bible, there are some definite ideas about diet. Why did God give those dietary laws in the Book of Leviticus? He wanted His people to be healthy. If your diet is not working for you to produce optimal health, what would you change? You might go to a nutritionist to evaluate your diet. That is not all bad. Why not go to God? The best nutritionist is God Himself! After all, God made everything! So, if God came and watched what you eat each meal of every day, what would He say to you? Obviously, the closer your food to the created order, the better. If you can grow your food in your backyard, you have control over what chemicals are put on your food and how it is grown. We have at times gone out in the back yard, picked lettuce, kale, and tomatoes for a salad, and walked into the house to prepare our salad. You can't get any fresher food than that!

When I went to college in central Missouri, I taught a Bible class at a small Lutheran church near the college. One of the members of the church was a farmer. He and his wife would invite me over for lunch after church every Sunday. The beef that was eaten was raised on their farm. The corn grew in their field. The bread came from wheat they had grown. They had a garden from which they got their vegetables for salads. Almost everything they ate, they grew! You can't get any fresher than that!

It may not be practical for many of us to grow our own beef or vegetables. But we do have choices in what we eat and where we eat. If you care about what you eat, you can find more healthy food. You can find food that is closer to the created order. Frankly, many people just don't care about what they eat. All they want to do is eat!

Adam was originally created to take care of the garden of Eden. He was free to eat from any of the trees in the garden except from the tree of the knowledge of good and evil (Genesis 2:16-17). When Adam and Eve fell into sin, they ate what God told them not to eat. It brought about their destruction. What I am implying is that God had a plan for Adam and Eve to eat things that would be good for them and help them to be healthy. God was their dietitian, so to speak. But they took matters into their own hands, ate what looked good to them, what was pleasing to their eyes, and the result was disaster. Could it be that God has a better plan for you and me when it comes to our diet? I think so.

A little confession here. I love potato chips. I do not like ice cream or sweets and rarely eat them. But I do eat potato chips! You know the old commercial that said, "I bet you can't eat just one!" Well, I do eat more than one. I usually eat about five to ten, no more than ten. All things are lawful for me, but not all things are beneficial! Do all things in moderation. Sometimes I skip lunch because I am busy doing other things. I find that about eight potato chips at 4 p.m. can help me make it until dinner time! So I am not advocating that we give up eating anything that is not healthy for us. All I am saying is eat unhealthy food in moderation.

So, what is unhealthy food? If the food you are eating is packaged, processed, or prepared only for the palette, the value it has for your physical well-being diminishes. It has been said that for some breakfast cereal foods, the box they come in would be more nutritious than the cereal in the box! Go to the farmer's market. They have farmer's markets even in big cities. Prepare the food yourself. Decide what you will cut out of your diet and what you will incorporate into your diet. Draw some boundaries around what you will eat and what you will not eat. Losing weight is a process. Losing weight a little at a time over a period of time is the key to weight loss. Some people exercise for a week, change their diet for a week, and wonder why they have not changed very much. Losing weight does not work that way! Try one simple dietary change over a specific period of time, let's say for a year. Give up sweets. Eat some kind of dark green vegetable with each dinner meal. Take a lunch to work rather than going to a fast-food restaurant. Instead of eating potatoes and bread, eat some kind of vegetable. Do it consistently. Add one simple change to your physical activity. Do it consistently. Do not become weary in well-doing (Galatians 6:9). Also, do not become weary in well-being! Over time, you will notice a big difference in your physical well-being.

My oldest son is a Chiropractor. His undergraduate degree is in nutritional sciences. He knows a great deal about good nutrition. My wife and I call him on a regular basis about nutrition. He has helped us understand about using coconut oil for cooking rather than olive oil. He has helped me understand that butter is not all that bad. He has encouraged us to use MCT oil for the brain. He has been a helpful resource.

Notice that when Jesus traveled from place to place, He walked. I have been to Israel and toured the Holy Land, and I can tell you there are many miles you have to travel from one place to another. Some of those walks Jesus and His disciples would take lasted all day long for several days in a row. Jesus had no gym membership. He did not have exercise machines at His house. But He stayed in shape. How? He kept moving. We live in a sedentary society. Here in Florida, people do not want to walk outside because it is hot and humid, and they may get sweaty. I guess that is one reason I do outside exercise in the morning. It is cooler. And I can take a shower before beginning the day's activities in the air conditioning! Some people in the Northern areas of the country do not walk outside in the winter. It is cold! I get that. If you live in a cold climate, walk on a treadmill with a computer screen in front of you. Watch scenes of Florida while you are walking! Just kidding. Watch a sermon while you walk! Have you noticed in health clubs they have several TV monitors in front of you? Watching something while you exercise can make the time pass quicker.

People are usually surprised when I tell them that I weighed more in 8th-grade than I did when I graduated high school. I weighed more when I was age fourteen than when I was age eighteen. When I was fourteen years old, I was terribly out of shape and overweight. When there was a president's fitness test (remember those?) where you would run around the track during physical education, I usually ended up either being last or next to last. When people were picked for teams in a game, be it kickball, softball, football, whatever sport it was, I was usually picked last. When I went into the school locker room, I would hide somewhere in the locker room to change my shirt. Why would I do that? Because I had breasts like a girl, and I was ashamed of that. I had a stomach that folded over in rolls. It was a painful time in my life. Looking back, I know that at that time in my life, I ate for comfort. Eating made me feel good about my life, at least for the moment.

In 9th-grade, I decided to join the football team. That was a good decision for me. I learned a great deal from being on a team of organized sports. I learned about sacrifice. I learned about the different positions in football. I learned that I was terribly out of shape. I was not very good at football. I actually played a total of five minutes in all the games during that season. Five minutes! Usually, I played at the very end of the game when it was obvious that my team would not win, or I played at the end of the game when it was obvious that my team was so far ahead, it was obvious we would win. You get the point. I learned a great deal from that time in my life. I learned that something had to change. I did not want to continue life being overweight.

After 9th-grade, my older brother talked to me about joining the high school wrestling team. He had already been on the wrestling team for a year. That meant, if I was going to wrestle, I had to lose weight. So in the summer between my 9th-grade and 10th-grade year, I starved myself. I ate the least amount possible. Not recommended, but it produced results for me. I would eat one bite of a meal and stop eating. Just enough to say I had eaten and to calm the gnawing in my stomach. It is probably easier for a young person to do this than someone who is older and has health problems. Anyway, I would not recommend it now! I ran around the block with a sweat suit on. A sweat suit is a plastic suit with elastic closures in the wrists, legs, and neck. Today this kind of weight loss program is not allowed in high school athletics. I remember taking the sweatsuit off and draining the water out of the suit. When the weather was rainy, I would turn on the hot water in the shower, create a steam room, and do burpees. A burpee is an exercise where you fall down on the floor on all fours, do a push-up, and jump up or stand up. That procedure would be one burpee. Try doing about fifty of them. I would not try it now! When I left 9th grade, I weighed 169 pounds. When I entered 10th grade, I wrestled at 132 pounds. I was surprised when other students saw me in the 10th grade and asked, "What happened to you over the summer?" Obviously, my physical appearance had changed. I looked totally different in 10th grade than I did in 9th grade. Do you know who noticed the weight loss the most? Not the coaches. Not the other guys. Who noticed it the most was the girls. I know how bad it hurts to be judged by others because you are overweight. I know what it is like to be accepted by others because you are thin. I determined at that point in my life that I would never go back to the overweight person I had been. I have worked out ever since that time. But I do not have a plastic suit anymore! Praise God! The point is, we can take control over our diet and our activity level. The question is, will we take control of our diet and our exercise?

Fasting: Fasting is a good way to loosen the grip food has on our lives. Jesus often fasted, and so did His disciples (Matthew 4:2, Matthew 6:16-18). Fasting has cleansing properties as well as spiritual benefits. When you are not living for food and instead, living for God, you put food in its place. We are to eat to live, not live to eat. Try a simple intermittent fast. Don't eat anything on a particular day until 5 p.m., then eat a regular meal. Notice I said a regular meal. That does not mean you reward yourself for going without food during that day and pig out at night! It is amazing how fasting can loosen the hold food has on us. You realize you can go a day without eating, and you will not die! Try fasting for one meal a day. Maybe you will skip lunch for a day. That is fasting. Another kind of fast is to use a smaller plate for your evening meal. What you are trying to do is to cut down on how much you eat at that meal. Don't go for seconds during a meal. Stop eating before you have the feeling of being full.

A disclaimer here. I am not your medical doctor, and it may not be wise for some people to fast. If you are a diabetic, for example, it may be better for you to eat a little bit of food several times during the day. Most of the time, a person's eating patterns have more to do with emotional needs than physical needs. Too often people eat to get some pleasure in their life. They have some sort of comfort food that makes them feel good about their life in the moment. The problem is that comfort food can be the go-to food of choice on a regular basis. Or they don't eat because they are too busy or stressed out to eat. Eating makes them feel ill. How much better to eat for the purpose of physical well-being rather than to cope with life's challenges? You are what you eat, and you eat because of who you are. If you are a new creation in Christ, you will care about what you eat and why you eat. Enough said.

Body Image: Many people struggle with their body image. They feel that there is something lacking in their body image. They look in the mirror at themselves and say, "Yuck!" They may think they are too tall, too short, too long of nose, too big of ears, too small in their breasts, too...well, you get the point. There can always be something about our bodies that we wish were different. Although I work out on a regular basis, I have never had a sixpack. I blame that on potato chips! I determined that my self-esteem would not be determined by whether I had a sixpack or not! I do have a sixpack, you just can't see it! It is there! Trust me! That is what I tell my wife. But I will not let a sixpack determine who I am as a person. You can do the same when it comes to your body image. Do you feel good about your body? Do you have some things about your body that show you are in good shape? Do you have a good body image?

If a person has a negative body image, it will block them from being what God wants them to be, a new creation. Can I give you a little suggestion? Make the best of what God has given you. God gave you your body. Yes, our physical appearance can be affected by the fall into sin, but in Christ, we can overcome most of those effects. Take what God has given you when He formed you in the womb, and do the best to take care of your physical appearance and physical well-being. Practice good physical and oral hygiene. Fix your hair on a regular basis. If you are a man and have a beard, trim your beard on a regular basis. Be proud of your body and how you look. It may take a little extra work, but it is well worth the effort.

At our church, Faith Lutheran in Merritt Island, Florida, we have a group home that we own and operate for mentally challenged people. I have learned a great deal being around the mentally challenged. Some of the residents of our group home are adults with Down Syndrome. They might not look like the majority of people, but they don't care about that. They don't really care how they look! They just want to love other people and to be loved by other people. We could learn from people who have Down Syndrome how to deal with our body image. We don't all look the same. We don't all have the same metabolism. We don't all have straight hair, blue eyes, and other so-called desired features, but we all have bodies that God created and that we can be good stewards of. Do the best with what you have.

I like to have a well-manicured yard. My wife and I do all the yard work at our house. Maybe it is due to me having a yard mowing business when I was younger, or maybe because I just like a nice yard. I work hard at keeping my yard looking nice. I feel the appearance of my yard says something about me. I don't have the most expensive house or the biggest house in town or the newest house, but I have a nice house. The yard is mowed on a regular basis. The sidewalks are edged. The bushes are trimmed. The weeds are pulled, well, most of the time. The point is, I want to do the best with what God has given me. You can drive through any neighborhood and tell who cares about their property and who neglects their property. You can tell a lot about people from their appearance as well. You can tell who cares about their appearance and who does not care about their appearance. Do the best with what you have been given. Do it unto the Lord and be pleased with that even if you don't look like a movie star!!

Rest: At the very beginning of creation, the Lord established the Sabbath. After six days of creation, God rested (Genesis 2:2-3). God did not rest because He needed to rest! He rested to establish a pattern for us. He did it because we need rest. The key when it comes to rest is to seek a balance to our lives. There is a time to work and a time to play. Some people do not know how to slow down and stop doing things. They feel guilty unless they work at something until they are so exhausted, they have to go to bed, or they crash. That is not a good way to live. Set aside a time to work, and work at your work with all your might (Colossians 3:23). But when it is time to stop and rest, stop and rest. Practice guilt-free resting. So simple, but so hard for some people. Incorporate into your life the time to enjoy other people. Incorporate into your life the time to enjoy God's creation. Incorporate into your lifetime to enrich your life through wholesome entertainment, podcasts, or a good book. That is what it means to balance your life. Is your life balanced? Even Jesus took time apart from the crowd, from the needs of people, in order to rest. One time He even took a nap in a boat in the midst of a storm! Jesus took a ministry nap! Rest does a body good!

I find that I am much more productive if I have a fresh mind and body. When I was working full-time as a pastor, I often came home for lunch. Early in my ministry, my wife and I decided that it would be best if we lived a short distance from the church. Not next door to the church, but within a five-to-ten-minute drive from the church. This way, I could come home for lunch, go to the children's school and sports activities, and still manage my responsibilities at the church. So, I would often come home for lunch. After I got a bite to eat at lunch, I would lay down for a few minutes in the bedroom to get quiet and to get in touch with my physical well-being and the Lord. If I fell asleep for a few minutes, that would be okay. When my son, Philip, was in ministry with me for a few years during the summers, he saw me doing this. He called it the ministry nap. He decided he would do the same thing! Resting is a time to regroup. I usually awake at 5 a.m., have devotions with my wife, do some exercise, get cleaned up, and am in the office by, at the latest, 7:30 a.m. If I have a meeting or appointments in the evening, which may go to 9 p.m., that ministry nap helps me regroup and be focused for the rest of the day.

There is also a sabbath rest when you can get away from your regular routine, if only for a day. It does not have to cost a lot of money to get away from your regular routine for a day. The key here is to get away. If you cannot go away for a night, go away for a whole day. Go sightseeing. Go to a park and take a walk and have a picnic. We have a boat. So, if we go boating early in the morning and fish for a couple of hours, we are getting away. We may then go for a boat ride and look at houses, expensive houses! Then we may go to an island and have lunch and wade in the water. It does not cost a great deal of money. I am sure that if you get creative, you can think of ways to get away from your regular routine, and it will not cost a great deal of money. Don't let finances stop you from getting away.

I had a pastor friend tell me one time, "I have not had a vacation for about twenty years." I told him that is pretty sick. It really shocked him. My pastor friend thought his work ethic was a badge of honor. I told him it only revealed that he was not balancing his life and was functioning at a diminished capacity. You need rest. You need time apart. Your business, your church, your house will continue to go on without you. When I go on a vacation, it takes me about three days to come down from my "being at work mentality" to a "being at rest mentality." It takes me about three days to flush out the adrenaline from my system so that I can relax and get used to doing very little or nothing. The first day of a vacation, I feel like I should be doing something that I am not doing. I feel guilty for not doing enough. The next day I realize that it is okay to not be doing something. The third day I begin to enjoy doing nothing except being with family and enjoying God's creation. I find that when I go away from my regular routine, I am ten times more productive when I come back. This is the secret to working smarter, not harder. It takes a few days to come down from an adrenaline high. It takes a few days to let the body cleanse itself of the toxins of your regular schedule and truly relax. Yes, that is even true for pastors!

God wants to be involved in all these physical well-being areas of our lives. You can be a new creation physically if you allow God to help you make a few simple changes.

1. How are you doing in your exercise routine? What exercise do you enjoy doing?
2. How are you doing with your diet? Is there anything in your diet you need to change?
3. Have you ever fasted? What was that like? How did you grow in your relationship with God because you fasted?
4. How are you doing when it comes to rest and getting away?

CHAPTER FIVE

Becoming a New Creation in Your Work

What are the different jobs you have done up to this point in your life? I have worked at a lawn mowing business, a custom bedding factory, as a painter, a janitor, a waiter, a bartender for catered parties (yuck!), and a roofer. Quite a resume! Where have you worked? I know some young people who have never worked outside of their homes. I know some people who worked at one job their whole life long. I know some people who have been stay-at-home mothers. A stay-at-home mother is one of the most taxing "jobs" in the world! If you worked at a lot of jobs, which one did you enjoy the most? If you worked at a job, you probably evaluated other positions on that job that you thought you would enjoy more. I have talked with some people who have felt stuck at their job. They worked at the same job for years, hated that job, but did not feel they could make any kind of change. That is sad. I have talked with other people who have enjoyed their job and said, "I can't believe I am getting paid to do something that I enjoy so much." Good for them. What about you? Where have you worked, and what was good about it? What was difficult about it?

One of the questions often asked during a job interview is, "What is your dream job?" Obviously, the interviewer is trying to find out about the job aspirations of the person seeking the job. What would you say is your dream job? Is your dream job one where you make a lot of money but don't have to do very much work? Is your dream job one where you can do what you want, travel a lot, and not have to manage other people? Is your dream job one where you believe you are making a positive difference in the world, no matter what the income is? What is your dream job?

We spend a great deal of our lives at work. If work is something that we abhor, our days will be drudgery and tiring. If work is a way that we please God, work can become something that enriches our lives and gives God glory. Which is it for you? Is your job a blessing or a curse?

We were created to work. What has made work difficult is the fall into sin. Before the fall happened in the garden of Eden, Adam was given the job of taking care of the garden (Genesis 2:15). Taking care of the garden was his joy and delight. He was taking care of the garden of Eden out of love for God. It was part of his worship of God.

When sin entered the world, all that changed. After the fall into sin, work became hard labor! Adam would sweat. I know something about sweat because I live in Central Florida! Part of the fall was that there would be thorns and thistles. In Florida, we would say there will be weeds. Lots of weeds! Because of sin, there would be parts of work that would be exacting and painful (Genesis 3:17-19). That is how many people view the whole of work today. A pain! But God wants to change that! Being a new creation in Christ means that work takes on a whole new meaning. We do not simply work for a paycheck. We work to honor God. We work for God.

The Word of God encourages us to work hard...heartily, as unto the Lord (Colossians 3:23). Who do you work for? What do you work for? God wants to redeem the value of work. No matter what your vocation, do it with all your heart. Your work is service rendered to the Lord.

One of the things I wanted to teach my children was to work hard. Notice I said I did not want to teach them to work too much, but when they were working, to do the best they could do and to give it their all. My wife and I have three boys and the fourth child, praise God, was a girl. I wanted my children to know the value of work.

Knowing that my children would want to get their driver's license when they were sixteen years old and to get a car as soon as possible, I gave them a way to do that. Work for it! I started telling them when they were thirteen or fourteen, "When you become sixteen, you will want to have a car. How do I know? I wanted a car when I was sixteen. It is a rite of passage. I will tell you how you can get a car when you are sixteen." I also wanted them to get a car at age sixteen so that I could monitor their car usage while they were still in my house. So, with my wife's agreement, we gave them chores to do around the house, which included monetary remuneration. We encouraged them to save for their first car. We told them we would contribute $1000 toward their first car. If they wanted a $1000 car, they did not need to work for anything more. If they wanted a better car, then they needed to work for it!

We helped them with a lawn moving business, driving them to mow yards and helping them with their equipment. When I heard of someone at the church who needed help with something like weeding, washing windows, and other household chores, I told my children about it before I told anyone else to see if they were interested. They usually responded with a "yes."

Our third son, Stephen, had saved over 5,000 dollars for his first car. That is pretty good for a sixteen-year-old! He bought a brand new Nissan Frontier for 13,000 dollars. He contributed 5000 dollars, we added 1000 dollars, and the remainder was a note that he faithfully paid until the truck was paid off. He learned the value of work. The message was clear: if you work hard, good things will happen. Hard work can help you reach your goals.

Another issue we had to deal with was car insurance. For teenage boys, car insurance is expensive! We did not want our children to think that driving a car was their right. Driving a car was a privilege. It costs money to own and drive a car. If they were responsible for the car and responsible for paying the costs of driving a car, they could own a car. My wife and I talked about how to help our children be responsible with a car and the costs of a car. We agreed that if they had a grade point average (GPA) of 3.75, we would pay all of their car insurance. All of it! That was a win-win. Not only would they apply themselves to their grades, but they would be able to qualify for scholarships and be able to apply to many different colleges if they had a high GPA. If they got a 3.5-3.75 GPA in a grading period, we would pay 75 percent of their car insurance. If they got a 3.25-3.5 GPA in a grading period, we would pay 50 percent of their car insurance. If they got a 3.0-3.25 GPA in a grading period, we would pay 25 percent of their car insurance. If they fell below a 3.0 GPA, we would not contribute anything to their car insurance. They would have to pay all the car insurance, or the car would remain parked at our house.

One grading period, one of my sons fell below a 3.0 GPA. He was working at a local retail store part-time. We told him that he had to turn over his paycheck each week toward the insurance. If he chose not to do this, the insurance would be canceled, and the car would be parked. Thankfully, at that time it was possible to take insurance off a car and still keep the car! It was very difficult for him to turn over his paycheck each week for that insurance. Guess what. The next grading period, his GPA rose to 3.5! Bad for his parents, but good for him! He never let his grades fall after that. Lesson learned. In fact, when he was a senior in high school, he really made his parents pay for his car insurance! We knew he had the ability. He just needed the right motivation.

My children learned how to work. Maybe not for the right motivation, but at least they understood the value of work. Many people today in the workforce are trying to figure out how they can do the least amount of work to get by. Their effort is not toward the work, but in how to get out of work! Not only is this displeasing to God, but it often leads to negative consequences in promotions, pay increases, and even in employment itself.

It takes eight years of schooling to be a Lutheran pastor: four years of college, and four years of seminary training, which includes one year of internship. To pay for college expenses, living expenses, and car expenses, I worked several different jobs. Primarily I worked in roofing. It was hard work. My first job at roofing paid by the hour. So, if you wanted to be paid more, you worked hard to merit a raise. After a month on my first roofing job, I went into the office of the owner. I asked for a raise. He was silent. I told him to ask the foreman how I was doing, that I was just as hard a worker as the rest of the roofers and just as fast. He raised his voice and said, "Get out of my office!" I did. The next Friday, I received a raise.

When I worked in St. Louis, Missouri, while attending the Seminary, I worked for a non-union roofing company. They had to pay comparable union wages to obtain workers. They paid by the amount of shingles that you laid. I made a lot of money there! I made enough money to finish school with no debt! However, it did take a toll on me. I have back problems that I attribute to hours of roofing! I have replaced my own roof, as well as the roof of many of my relatives. I have replaced the roofs of people that were in need and could not afford for a roofing company to replace their roof. If you are roofing with me, I can tell in a short while whether you know how to work!

In the summer of 1979, I lived with the family of one of my classmates in South St. Louis while I worked for a roofing company. The father in that family owned and operated a plumbing business. He had been very successful in his company. Sometimes at breakfast, he would look out the window of his house and quote Proverbs 26:13-16, which states, "There is a lion on the road. Yes, I am sure there is a lion out there!" He was just joking around, of course. The lazy person does not want to go to work because there just might be a lion outside. The lazy person looks for any excuse not to work. The verse in Proverbs goes on to say, "As a door swings back and forth on its hinges, so the lazy person turns over in bed. Lazy people take food in their hand but don't even lift it to their mouth. Lazy people consider themselves smarter than seven wise counselors!" Being a new creation in Christ means you are not lazy. You work hard at your work.

As a young minister, I realized there was no time clock to punch in each day. I realized that there was such trust in the pastor that he could get away with anything when it came to his work ethic. As a pastor, you are your own boss, so to speak. What I realized when I started work as a pastor was that God was my boss. God was watching. God may not reward me monetarily for hard work as a pastor, but He was interested in how I handled the trust I had been given. To be honest, as a young pastor, I worked too much. I was gone from the family too much. I had to learn how to work smarter. I had to learn how to accomplish more in less time. I had to learn how to budget my time. I had to learn how to balance my time between rest, family, friends, and work. I had to learn how to delegate tasks to other people and take my hands off of the ones I had delegated. I had to learn how to trust people to do what I asked them to do. I made lots of mistakes. But I learned to work not harder but smarter. I also learned that you don't work for money as a pastor. To work for money in ministry is a big mindset mistake. Money is a poor taskmaster. I set a standard to work for the Lord and to please Him and Him only. You know, God does not get upset when you budget time for your family. God does not get upset when you only work forty or fifty hours per week, rather than sixty or seventy hours per week. In fact, I believe God is pleased if you balance the different aspects of your life rather than working too much.

Many people work too much. They get caught up in a job that pays well. They get used to receiving and spending the great pay they earn, and they feel trapped. They feel they have to bow down to their employer or lose the life of opulence they have gained. Maybe it would be better, even more God-pleasing, to work less, make less, buy less, and have more time for the things that really matter. Things like family, healthy living, or seeking after God.

"Whistle While You Work" is a song featured in the 1937 Disney film "Snow White and the Seven Dwarfs." Snow White decides to clean the house of the dwarfs while they are away. She was thinking that the dwarfs will be so grateful that she cleaned their house, they will let her stay with them. The forest animals get involved and help her as she sings. What is the message of that song? Do what you can, when you can, to be the best you can. But remember the song with this line, "Where never is heard a discouraging word"? That line can be more than lyrics to a song. You can enjoy your work if you approach it with the proper mindset. Whistle while you work; don't grumble.

Notice the big picture regarding work. It may seem like what you are doing is not really making much of a difference in the world. Not true. When you see your work as joined to the work of others and as something used by God to accomplish His purpose, your work takes on a whole new significance. It may seem like you are not being paid enough for the work you are doing. That may be true. Rather than grumbling about a low-paying job, or begrudging your employer, do your work for God. God will reward you for a job well done. Remember what the Lord said to some who arrived in heaven, "Well done, good and faithful servant!" (Matthew 25:23) To hear these words from God is a great reward. When all is said and done, can you say, "I have only done my duty?"

Are you becoming a new creation in Christ in your work? Here are some questions to help you explore your answer to that question. Be honest. Remember, God already knows the answer.

1. Are you a hard worker?
2. Have you balanced your work with other areas of your life?
3. Who or what are you working for?
4. How can you become a new creation in Christ in your work?

CHAPTER SIX

Becoming a New Creation Financially

A part of your body really becomes important when it is hurting. If you stub your toe on a chair in the middle of the night, and it throbs with pain, that toe will become very important to you at that moment. Normally that toe is not even thought about. It is just a toe. But when that toe is hurt, it will scream for attention! The same is true when it comes to money. If money is important to you, and you feel a great deal of distress or hurt about money, then money will become the loudest screamer in your life. If money, or the lack of money, is not an issue for you, you may not think about it very much. Whether a toe is hurt or not, toes are important! Whether money is a sore spot for you or not, money is important! You cannot stand very well if a toe is hurting or absent. You cannot function very well without a toe. Neither can you stand very well in life if money is a problem for you, or if you ignore the impact of money on your life. Becoming a new creation in Christ means you care deeply about the effect money is having on our life.

It is much harder to manage your finances when you don't know how much money you will make each month. I know what it is like to not have very much money. I know what it is like to wonder how you are going to be able to pay your bills. In the fourth year of my seminary education, I was married and had one child. I worked as a waiter in downtown St. Louis, and my wife worked as an organist for a nearby church. I did some small roofing jobs when I could and when they were available. Our income was very fluid. We did not know from week to week how much money we would have. We had to juggle the bills until we knew we had enough money to pay them. It was not easy. I don't know what it is like to live on a limited income. We had to put our faith in God to provide what was needed to pay our bills and to eat. And God did provide what was needed.

In my first few years of being a pastor, our income was small, but the amount was stable. We knew what money was coming in, so we could adjust our spending accordingly. Sometimes, after I would deduct all the bills we had to pay from our income, my wife would ask me how much money we had to purchase groceries. At that point, I had finished four years of college and four years of seminary. I had a master's degree. I told her sometimes during those years, "We have $25 dollars for groceries until the next month." We had to decide how to spend that $25 in the best way possible to have food to eat. I know what it is like to not have very much money.

When I came to the church where I was a pastor in 1988, our income was very limited. Actually, we accepted a reduction in pay to come to that church. We had four children at the time. The children who went to public school received government-subsidized lunches. To supplement our income, I did some small roofing jobs on Sunday afternoon and on Monday, my day off. At the end of the first year of serving at that church, one of the Elders in the church said to me, "Pastor, we gave you a fifteen percent raise because we don't want you to have to do roofing to provide for your family." I was extremely grateful for that raise! I know what it is like to not have very much money. It is not easy. You have to put your faith in God to make it!

Money is important. You can't live very well in this world without some amount of money. Money also defines what is important to us. Better said, how we view our money and how we use our money defines what is important to us. So, I want to get personal with you. What does your use of your money say about you? If I looked at your bank statement or your credit card statement, I could easily tell you what is important to you. How we use our money says something about our relationship with God. A person who is becoming a new creation in Christ will steward their money in such a way that God is pleased about the decisions they make about what they do with the money God has entrusted to them.

Does God care about our money? Not really. He cares about our attitude about money. God already owns our money. You don't take anything with you when you die. You leave all your earthly possessions here in this life. You leave it all here. What you have in this life is on loan to you from God. What God cares about the most is our love for Him. He wants our love for Him to be reflected in how we use our finances and how we think about our finances. Jesus said it well, "You cannot love God and mammon (money). You cannot serve two masters. If you love one, you will hate the other." (Matthew 6:24) What was He saying? Love me, not the things of this earth. Use the things of this earth to show your love for me. Too often we switch the price tags. We use people and love things. We use God and love money. What God wants is that we love Him and use our money to show that we love Him. It is the love of money that is the root of all evil (1 Timothy 6:10). If there is a clear way to discern whether we are becoming a new creation in Christ, it will be seen in our attitude about money and things. I would dare say that all of us, at least all of us in America, have some growing to do in this area. I know that I do.

In the medical profession, x-rays and MRIs are used to look beneath the surface of our bodies to see what is going on inside our bodies. If you intend to go on an airplane trip, you will likely need to go in an x-ray machine, lift your hands up, and be scanned. Airport security utilizes the x-ray machine to see if you have anything hidden on your body that is not allowed on the airplane. If you want to look below the surface of your life and discern what your real attitude is about money, look at what you do when it comes to your offerings to the Lord and His church. What you do with your offering reveals what is really in your heart when it comes to your attitude about money. When we only had twenty-five dollars for our groceries, we still had planned to give an offering to the Lord. We put our offering to God before our own needs. And God provided what we needed.

When the offering plate is passed in church, does God have to pry your offering from your hands? If you do not go to church, how much do you really give to God and His kingdom? Experience tells me that those who are not connected to the body of Christ in a local church give very little to the work of the kingdom of God. So, is there room to grow? You bet! I am not saying you have to become a monk in order to be like Christ. That is, to take a vow of poverty. What I am saying is that God wants to be in control of how we use our money. God wants to be honored in how we spend our money. God wants us to put Him first in our financial decisions. This is not natural, and it is not easy. It will take a work of God for us to make changes in this area. It will take a desire on our part to be new creations in Christ for us to change how we make decisions about money. When you think about our use of money in our lives, it is like what God said to Cain in the book of Genesis: "Sin (instead of anger, let's say money) is crouching at the door and it seeks to master you" (Genesis 4:7). That is not to say that money is sinful. It is to say that how we make decisions about money can be self-centered and, therefore, sinful. If you want to know someone's true spiritual condition, just look at their checkbook. Their checkbook will reveal what is really important to them.

None of us wants everyone to know what we spend our money on. We say it is a private thing. Yet God looks at our checkbook all the time. There are no secrets before Him. God knows whether we are like the widow in the temple who gave all that she had or like the hoarder who says, "Look what great things I have amassed for myself." Stay with me here. I am not saying that I have arrived at spiritual maturity when it comes to the use of money. I am saying that I am in the process of becoming more like Christ. Sometimes it is very difficult, especially in our affluent world. I hope you would say the same and say that you are on the journey to become a new creation in Christ regarding your finances.

First of all, let's look at some money pitfalls. I encourage you to honestly evaluate how you are doing in each of these areas. Let God be your financial advisor. That means, as God looks at how you are managing your finances, He has the right to say, "This is not good. Let's change that." Are you ready?

Pitfall number one: *Not enough margin.*

Not having enough margin means that you either live paycheck to paycheck, never having enough to get by or to do anything more, or you have not reduced your expenses in proportion to your income so that you have some margin. When you pay all your bills, you have nothing left over, and even worse, you can't pay all your bills. Here is a truth that most people will not recognize. Usually, spending increases to use up anyone's available income. If you make 30,000 dollars a year and, you spend 30,000 dollars a year or more, you have no margin. The amazing thing is that if you made 30,000 dollars a year and, through the blessing of God, you were blessed with 50,000 dollars a year, the tendency is that you would spend all of that, if not more, and have no margin. If you made 100,000 dollars a year, you would spend all of that or more and still have no margin. You get the picture. Why do we do that? We feel like we went without some "essentials" for some time, and now we have been blessed. We think, why not do some of those things I could not do before? Spending increases to the level of our available income. The point is, where does it stop? For some people, it never stops. They have no margin, no matter what their income level is.

About ten years ago, I was in my middle fifties. We lived in an older house built in 1964. Since our children were grown, out of college, and on their own, we decided we were going to upgrade our house to a newer house. What could be wrong with having a newer house? Surely God had blessed us. Would it not be God-honoring to show to the world how God had blessed us by getting a more modern house? A newer house would be a testimony of how good God is. Interesting how we think, isn't it? So we started looking at houses. If we sold our house and purchased a newer house, we would have a higher mortgage. Our current mortgage was close to being paid off. Since we had lived in our old house for so long, if we purchased a new house, our property taxes would quadruple. It dawned on us to ask the question, "Is it our goal to leverage our income into debt or to stay where we are and use the margin for other things?" Tough question. Get the picture? Our current house had four bedrooms, and we only needed one. Our current house had a pool. Our current house had completely been renovated inside and out by my wife and myself. Our current house had a concrete slab behind a fence where we could store our boat. Yes, we have a boat. Our current house was at a great location for shopping. Our current house had served us well and could serve us well until life's end. So why would we cash all that in to get a newer house? Because we could. Away with margin.

Well, older houses have some problems. Sometimes the plumbing fails because it is old. Electrical problems arise because, well, the house is old. We only had a one-car garage. Feel sorry for us? You get the point. The grass is always greener on the other side, but it can get weeds, bugs and still needs to be mowed. A newer house did not mean all the problems of an older house would be gone. So we decided to stay in our old house. That created some margin.

You can do the same margin dance with cars. Do you keep driving an older car that works just fine, or do you think you need to purchase a new car with a note? Away with margin. You can plug anything into the equation. If spending increases to suck up available income, there will be no margin. But, as income increases and you seek to keep spending constant, there will be margin. When there is margin, God says, "This is what I have been waiting for! Now that I have blessed you, you can be a blessing to others!" If you don't have any margin, take some steps to create some. Creating margin is one step to becoming a new creation in Christ financially.

Pitfall number two: *To have no accountability.*

We don't like accountability! One reason people do not like to have a budget is that they don't like accountability. A budget reeks of control. A budget will cramp our style. A budget will kill spontaneity, or so we think. If the money is there, why not enjoy it? When we are accountable to someone, we have a plan that has been made, and we know that we will have to answer about how we stayed with the plan. Many married people have a lot of arguments about money because one or both of them is trying to keep the other person accountable! How much more different is it when you go to God, tell Him your plan, and answer to Him about how you will keep the plan.

Indeed, we are all accountable to God. God can and does ask us how we did with what He gave us. One day we will stand before God in eternity. God will hold us accountable for how we handled the talents He gave to us in this life. Not that our use of money has anything to do with our salvation. Jesus already took care of our salvation. Our use of money reveals whether we trust God to provide. Our use of money is our response to God's salvation. Our use of money reveals whether we are grateful to God for all He has done for us. He already knows what we have done with our financial resources. God wants us to be honest about our money management. If you have not been wise with your financial management, make some changes. Make the changes now. These changes show that you want to become a new creation in Christ financially.

Some people have a financial advisor who holds them accountable. Why not enlist God as your financial advisor? Some people have creditors that hold them accountable. After all, when you take on a debt, don't you sign an agreement that makes you accountable? I think the best auditor is God. Involve Him in the plan, sign on with Him, and go to Him regularly with a financial status report.

I have been talking about accountability in our finances. I will give you a personal example about financial accountability. Some years ago, the Internal Revenue Service (IRS) sent us a notice that my wife and I were being called in for an audit. The letter said that we were selected for an audit at random. They decided to take a detailed look at two years of our tax returns. I said, "Okay, Lord, what are you teaching us here?" It was an interesting process. We took all of our records to the judgment hall. One IRS worker sat across the table from us and asked us a myriad of questions. Another IRS worker sat behind that worker by a wall with a notepad and took notes. Whew! At least they did not record the whole thing! After four appointments, they were satisfied with our answers. Since I have always prepared my own taxes, I was able to state why we did what we did in our tax returns according to IRS law. We did not do anything that was unlawful, but boy, did we feel accountable! We ended up owing less than a hundred dollars for two years of tax audits. Lesson learned! If you can afford it, hire someone to prepare your taxes. Let them be accountable! When we were first married, we could not afford to pay someone to prepare our tax returns. Since I had been preparing our taxes for years, we had to face the bench on our own. Lesson learned! When you do your taxes, do them as if God were watching, and believe that He is very interested in what you are doing. The fact of the matter is, God is watching, and He is very interested!

Be accountable to God now about what you do with your money, or be accountable when you stand before the judgment seat of God. Your choice.

Pitfall number three: *To not practice sacrificial giving.*

Obviously, in order to practice sacrificial giving, we need to have margin! If you are sacrificial in giving and have no margin, you will not eat! Sacrificial giving is the way God works. God gave you everything you have, even though you don't always use it in the way He would like. He gave you all you have, and if you have no margin or are not sacrificial in your giving, you have squandered what He has given you. Kind of like the prodigal son (Luke 15)! In this story, the father gave his son his share of the inheritance, even though he was not entitled to it.

That son went to a far country and squandered his inheritance. God gives sacrificially to us in that He gave His only begotten Son into death for us on the cross so that we might receive as a gift, free and clear, His forgiveness and life everlasting. It cost Him a great deal. It cost us nothing. Therefore, if you want to be a new creation in Christ, you will be like God and grow in the practice of sacrificial giving. Ouch!

Have you been sacrificial in giving to others in their time of need? My answer? Sometimes. I have given cars away to people in need. There is some sacrifice in that, but not much. A sacrifice means your giving cost you something. If a gift costs us nothing, then the gift means nothing. I can give someone 100 dollars, but if I am a millionaire, there is little sacrifice involved. If I give someone 100 dollars and that means I cannot go out to eat for the rest of the month or go to a movie, that involves some sacrifice. If I give someone in need 1000 dollars, and that means I cannot go on a nice vacation, that involves a sacrifice. Too often, we give from leftovers and not sacrificially.

What about when it comes to the support of the work of God? Is your offering to a church a sacrifice to you? It is my observation that usually those who are lower on the income scale give more sacrificially to the Lord than those who are wealthy. Someone can give 100 dollars a month in their offering, and that gift is more in proportion to their income than someone who gives 1000 dollars a month in their offering. For some people, 1000 dollars a month is no sacrifice at all. To some, 100 dollars a month is a great sacrifice. If you want to be more sacrificial in your giving, what would you give up in order to give more? Tough question. I told you this would not be easy. Jesus gave His all. Thankfully, God does not require that of us. He does want to know if He is important enough to us that we would give something up, to sacrifice, in order to give to the work of His kingdom or to those in need.

Years ago, when my children were young, we would go to what was then known as Ski Island. Ski Island is a little island by the Port Canaveral Lock. We would go there to water ski, wakeboard, and tube. If we went there on a weekend, there would be a great deal of boats on the island. It was obvious that many of those boat owners were not interested in water sports. They came to Ski Island "thirsty," if you know what I mean. Often, we would leave some people in our group on the island and take just a few out in the boat for the water sports, then come back to the island to exchange the people who wanted to do water sports from those who wanted a break.

Let me paint a picture of the contrast. Our boat was an old boat I had purchased from my brother, who taught marine mechanics at a local high school. It ran great! It looked like a relic from days gone by. My feeling about a boat is, if it floats and runs, what is wrong with that? When we would pull up on the island, it was obvious that most of the people at the island had spent a great deal more money for their boats than we had done for ours. Get the picture? My children called that boat the affectionate name of "Old Blue." Kind of like the dog called "Old Yeller."

One time, when we were waiting at the island to take off with a fresh group of people, one of my sons said, "Dad, why don't we have a nice boat like the rest of these people?" All my children must have been thinking the same thing because they all paused, like an E. F. Hutton moment and looked at me, wondering what I would say. I paused for a moment. It was a moment of truth. I said, "We have decided that God is more important than a nice boat. If we did not give as much of an offering to the Lord, we could easily afford a nice boat. But I am willing to use this boat as long as we can give our offering to the Lord. That is why we do not have a nicer boat." They nodded. There was silence. Boat? Or God? The decision was one of obedience to God for me and my wife. That is the spirit of sacrifice.

Pitfall number four: *To have no savings plan.*

If you have no margin, you will not have much savings. If you do not have accountability and spend your income according to the feelings of the moment, rather than according to a plan, you will not have much in savings. If you have savings, you will be ready for a rainy day. If you have savings, you will be able to be sacrificial in your giving. If you have savings, you will be able to use the power of cash for major purchases.

Most of the time in our married life, we purchased used cars. Why? Because we could pay cash for them, and I could work on them to fix them when they were broken. As I became older, I decided it was time to purchase a car that was new so that I would not need to work on it! So, when we were ready to purchase a new car, a truck, I did a great deal of research online about the kind of vehicle I wanted and how much I wanted to pay for it. Car dealers love it when buyers do that! Not! I decided I wanted a Ford F150, what engine I wanted, and what features I wanted. My wife decided what colors we would not have. So, it was a partnership! She did not want a black or a red truck. That narrowed down the selection a bit. Then I emailed eight local dealerships and told them what truck I wanted, what features I wanted, and what I wanted to pay for it. I told them that if they could not get close to the price I was willing to pay, don't waste my time. One of them emailed me back. I ended up buying that truck for close to the price that I wanted because I was able to pay cash for the truck. And I was willing to walk away if they would not work with me. It is freeing to not have a note, to not pay interest on a loan. You can only do that if you have a savings plan, stick with it, and have a goal you are willing to save for.

God has stored up for His children an inheritance that is beyond price. It is an inheritance that cannot spoil or fade. That inheritance is heaven itself. God has already paid for us to go there. He paid for us to go to heaven with the death and resurrection of His Son, Jesus Christ. God had a plan to bless us eternally. In that sense, be like God. Have a plan and be willing to sacrifice to achieve that plan. Be a saver.

God does not want us to be burdened about money. He has promised to meet our needs, and He has given us principles whereby we can be wise with our money. Therefore, generally speaking, if you are burdened about money, you probably are not following God's plan.

God does not promise you that you will be financially wealthy. Look at Jesus. Jesus sent His disciples to fish in order to get money to pay their taxes. When the disciples pulled up a fish, there was a coin in the mouth of the fish (Matthew 17:24-27). I am still waiting for that to happen when I go fishing! Jesus had no place to lay His head. Jesus was buried in a borrowed tomb. Furthermore, Jesus had done no burial planning! The acquisition of money was not His goal. He came to seek and to save the lost! Keep in mind that it is not sinful to be wealthy. Look at Solomon in the Old Testament. Solomon was very wealthy. However, it is a sin to live for money and not for God.

God wants you to be content. As I have thought about contentment, I can see that tension exists. There is a tension between trying to better yourself, therefore, to some degree, not being content and not accepting your position in life. On the other hand, being content means that you are satisfied with what you have and accept your position in life. So, do you strive for more, or are you content with what you have? Both. Being content is not synonymous with laziness. But the person who has contentment will not get stressed out about his/her present position. They may have goals. They will strive to meet those goals. They will celebrate when they reach those goals. But they will not fall apart emotionally when they do not reach them. They will not strive for an increase in money to the point that their health and relationships suffer. They will be content. When you are content, you can strive to do better, but the striving to do better does not control your life. Godliness with contentment is great gain (1 Timothy 6:6).

Have you ever made some bad decisions when it comes to your management of money? I know I have. Early in our marriage, we bought a timeshare in Hot Springs, Arkansas. Because our money was tight, we had to get a note to pay for the timeshare. We could not afford the monthly note. We could not even afford the yearly maintenance fee. We decided to back out of the deal. I told the company that we had made a mistake and that we simply did not have enough money to afford a timeshare. They told me that breaking the contract might be reported to the credit bureau and affect our credit. I told them we did not have the money and that we had to do what we had to do, and they would have to do what they felt they needed to do. We backed out of the timeshare contract. They never reported us to the credit bureau. I am thankful for that! I don't like breaking contracts, but in this case, we had no choice. Sadly, buying a timeshare was not the only money mistake we have made. I am not going to tell you the rest of them! My guess is that you have made some bad money decisions as well. Put those decisions in the past and move on.

It is important if you are married that you have agreement about how you spend your money. If you make a bad decision regarding your money, but you were both in agreement about the bad decision, you really cannot blame one another. You own the decision together. But, if one person makes the decision, and they do it without consulting their partner, when the bad decision comes to light, trust in the relationship is damaged. I know someone who was "playing" in the stock market. They did not tell their partner what they were doing. They lost a great deal of money in the stock market. When the bills came due, and it was revealed that the money was gone, there was a day of reckoning. Thankfully, this couple practiced confession and forgiveness and picked up the pieces, and moved on. The point is, make your money decisions together, even the bad ones!

God wants to remove our guilt if we realize that we have been poor money managers. That is why Jesus went to the cross. He went to the cross to provide for our forgiveness. But once we are forgiven, God wants us to make some changes in our lives. In order to evaluate whether there are changes that need to be made regarding your money management, answer the following questions.

1. What changes will you allow God to make in your life so that you can be more of a new creation in Christ in your finances?
2. Do you have some margin? How much margin?
3. Are you accountable for some kind of spending plan?
4. Do you have some kind of savings plan?
5. Do you ever sacrifice your desires in order to give to God or to others?
6. Are you content with what you have?
7. Are you becoming a new creation financially?

CHAPTER SEVEN

Becoming a New Creation in Our Sexuality

Old habits can, at times, be very difficult to change. It is only by the power of God that we can change those habits. Some people have had the habit of pleasing themselves sexually through masturbation. Some people have the habit of seeking sexual pleasure through the use of pornography. For some people, looking at pornography has become more than a habit, it is an addiction. Some people have tried to get their sexual needs met through illicit sex. These habits are not what God wants for our sexual expression. These habits are not healthy. When you go down these paths, it can be very difficult to make a change. But not impossible. Change in our dysfunctional sexual patterns only happens by the power of God. Are there any sexual patterns in your life that you would like to change? Do you feel trapped in your sexual desires? Do you feel guilty about your sexual choices? I have seen some people live with a partner without being married. That relationship breaks up, and they start a new relationship. That relationship breaks up, and they begin a new relationship. Our culture does not give us a very healthy picture of what it means to be in a healthy sexual relationship. In our culture, we see people in serial relationships. In our culture, we see people parading same-sex relationships as if that is normal. In our culture, we see people having affairs. If there is any area of our life that needs God's help in order for us to be new creations in Christ, it is our sexuality. There is great pressure in our society to do what sexually feels good in the moment. When have you felt pressured by society to behave sexually in a certain way? When have you given in to the feelings of the moment to be sexual, even when it is not the way God wants you to be sexual? Are you bold enough to share that with others who are on the journey to becoming new creations in Christ?

A young man takes a young girl on a date. They are both excited because when he asked her to go on a date, she said, "yes." There has already been some attraction between them, some sexual electricity. He has noticed she is gorgeous. She has noticed he is "fine." He is handsome, nice, respectful, and easy to talk with. They have already had times together, laughing, working together on school projects. At the agreed-upon time, he picks her up for their first date. After getting a bite to eat, he drives her to a public park. It is dark, and it seems that there is no one else at the park. As they sit in the car, he pulls her over to be closer to him. He takes her hand in his hand. It feels good for both of them to hold hands. It feels a little exciting. After a while, he leans over to kiss her. She leans over to kiss him. It feels good to kiss. It feels a little exciting to kiss. Their bodies begin to respond to the excitement of the moment.

Without really realizing it, their hearts begin to beat faster, and their blood begins to flow quicker. Their bodily sensations feel enhanced. Slowly, he begins to caress her shoulders and arms as they kiss. It feels good to be caressed. It enhances the excitement. Slowly, he moves his hand to her chest. She enjoys being caressed. It makes her feel special, wanted, loved.

Okay, enough of that story. I made it up. Where do you think this story is going? Have you ever been in this kind of situation? What would you do? What did you do?

When was your first sexual experience? I am referring to your first sexual experience with someone of the opposite sex. Was that experience a good experience, or was it a bad experience? It is sad to say, but too often true: most young people experiment with sex. Some young people experiment with sex multiple times. I am not saying this is what God wants. What I am saying is that people have sexual needs and want to explore their sexual feelings. What God wants is that we are patient and wait to experience sex when we are married.

In marriage, two people can experience fantastic sex. That raises a question. What is fantastic sex? Is fantastic sex having sex with a different partner each night? Is fantastic sex when both people are full of passion? How would one have fantastic sex their whole life long? What would God say is fantastic sex? Does God want to be involved in our sexuality? You bet. God wants you to have the best sex life you can imagine. Do you want that? Are you willing to let God show you how to have the best sex life that is possible? The desire to let God teach you about sex and lead you toward a fantastic sex life is part of becoming a new creation in Christ. Later in this chapter, I will share the sex trinity. These three things are very important things to practice if you want to have fantastic sex.

It is important to becoming a new creation in Christ sexually to understand and learn to manage the sexual differences between men and women. Many women in particular like reading romance novels or watching what is known as "chic flicks." Many men do not like reading romance novels or watching "chic flicks." Why the difference? God created men and women different in their sexual response. Because of this difference, there is sexual tension between men and women that can be good, or it can be bad. Most women want to be romanced. They want to feel that the man is passionately in love with them. I get that. Most men want either a one-night stand or what is called a "quickie." I get that. Most women want a romantic invitation, a romantic dinner, a romantic evening, a romantic conversation, some romantic touching, some romantic kissing before they are willing to commit themselves sexually. I get that. Generally speaking, men want sex. Men want the thrill of the moment and then the thrill of a happy ending. I get that. Do you see where the tension lies? God has made us different as male and female. And that is okay. Right? As long as we respect the differences between males and females.

Sex is a beautiful creation of God. We are sexual beings. God made us that way. In the beginning of creation, the Bible says that God made them male and female (Genesis 1:27, Mark 10:6-9). The first man was Adam. The first woman was Eve. Each of them was distinctly different from the other. They were different anatomically, and they were created different emotionally too. That was God's design. If male and female were both the same in their emotional response to intimacy, the sexual experience would be boring. No, God has made male and female different. By design. For the good of both the male and female.

Basic anatomy reveals that a man and a woman were made different from one another, and they were made for one another. Need I explain further? A man and a man, according to anatomy, were not made for one another sexually. A woman and a woman were not made for one another sexually. I know this may not sit right with some people, but simple observation of human anatomy reveals this is true. That is all I am going to say about that! Three times in the Bible God gives His pattern for marriage. You can find them in the very beginning of the Bible in the book of Genesis, in the words of Jesus in the Gospel of Matthew, and in the teaching of the Apostle Paul in the book of Ephesians. Obviously, becoming one flesh refers to the sexual union. You see these words at the beginning of creation, from the words of Jesus, and from the teaching of The apostle Paul. The point is that God's plan did not change through time. People have changed the plan of God. God's plan is for one man and one woman to be joined as husband and wife in a life-long commitment. Period. That is the plan. Anything beyond that is not God's plan.

Sex between a man and a woman is beautiful in the right context. A fire in a fire pit or a fireplace is beautiful. A fire burning down a house is not beautiful; it is destructive. Sex between a married couple, a man and a woman, is intended to be beautiful. Sex outside of the boundary of marriage is destructive. Why? There is very little commitment between a man and a woman when sex takes place outside of marriage. Some people like sex outside of the commitment of marriage because their focus is on themselves and their own pleasure, not on a committed relationship with their spouse. Sex outside of the commitment of marriage is destructive because sex outside of marriage brings shame. Sex outside of the commitment of marriage opens the door to the possibility of sexually transmitted diseases. Sex outside of marriage can affect the life of the people involved and the life of many other people because there could be a pregnancy. Sex outside of marriage is destructive because it displeases God.

Sex in marriage is beautiful because it is a picture of Jesus' love for the church. The apostle Paul makes this comparison in Ephesians, Chapter 5. Sex in marriage is designed by God to be the ultimate in intimacy, closeness, and sharing that two people can experience. When God took a rib from Adam in the very beginning and created a woman from the rib, God presented the woman, Eve, to the man. Adam said, "She will be called woman for she was taken out of man" (Genesis 2:23). I sometimes have said in a wedding message that in the Hebrew language, the word woman can be translated, WOW-MAN! Let me say that is not really what the Hebrew language means. Needless to say, Adam was very excited! Therefore, sex in marriage is meant to be thrilling, exciting, fulfilling, engaging, and whatever other wonderful word you can think of. Adam and Eve were naked and not ashamed. It is to be that way in marriage.

Let me pose a probing question. How is it going in your marriage sexually? Is there room for growth in this area? Becoming a new creation in Christ sexually is accomplished in marriage. The unity of the Trinity is evidenced in the unity between a husband and wife. In the Trinity, the Father, Son, and Holy Spirit are separate persons, but one in purpose, desire, and essence. Sex in marriage is where two people become one flesh. Husband and wife are separate persons, but they experience in the sexual relationship a small part of the unity of the Trinity. God designed it that way. It is a wonderful experience. Do you have that kind of intimate connection in your marriage? Let me be frank: very few people do. Yet, there is good news! There is room for growth! You can be a new creation in Christ sexually!

When my wife and I would lead marriage seminars, we would place in the conference room a question box and some slips of paper. The couples that attended the seminar could anonymously write a question about marriage and put it in the box. At different points in the seminar, I would reach into the box and pull out a question. I would read the question and then deal with the issue that had been raised on the slip of paper. Guess what questions came up the most? Questions about sex. That was an indicator to me that at least some of the couples present were struggling with their sexual relationship. When we led a marriage seminar, we would always do an hour-long presentation on sexual relationship. Then we would give some questions to the couples and ask them to go somewhere alone and talk about the questions. I had a rule in the marriage seminars. The rule was the couples could not share something about their marriage with the larger group of people unless they had their partner's permission. I did not want anyone to hear their partner say something about their marriage that their partner would be hearing for the first time in the large group. Needless to say, that rule probably stopped a lot of people from sharing intimate things with the group. But that rule built trust in the marriage relationships of those couples. In those marriage seminars, I did not want anyone throwing his/her mate under the bus in front of the group!

When I would do marriage counseling, I would work on making changes with the couple so that the cycle of the hurt they were experiencing could be disrupted, and good things could begin happening in their relationship. At some point in the counseling process, as good things started happening, I would tell the couple that good communication is great. Negotiating differences is great! Problem-solving is great! But I would say to them in the counseling process that we are fooling ourselves if we think that their marriage is doing great if there is not very much happening in their sexual relationship. So, I would then ask them what had been going on in their sexual relationship. In answer to that question, I have heard couples say they have had sex maybe one time in the last three years. I do not get shocked anymore when I hear that. I have heard it, or something similar, too many times. Lesson learned, there is room for growth! If that is the norm in your marriage, do something about it. Go to counseling. Read a Christian book on sex. Listen to some podcasts on the internet. I would tell the married couples in the marriage seminars I led that if they are not having sex at least a couple of times during the week, you might want to discuss the frequency/fulfillment that is going on in your sexual relationship. Most couples do not talk about their sexual relationship. Couples work on their sexual relationship by talking with each other about their hurts, desires, needs. I would tell them that if at least once a month, both of them would not say their sexual experience was very fulfilling, something was wrong in their sexual relationship. In my counseling experience, this is a baseline. Do not settle for less in what God has intended for you sexually. Also, do not seek to get your sexual needs met outside of your marriage. Work diligently on becoming a new creation in Christ in your sexual relationship. Fix what is broken. Do not delay.

One way couples can work on fixing their sexual relationship is to read some books on the sexual relationship. There are many Christian books and internet help on sex in marriage. The problem is that many people do not use these resources. I used to ask the premarital couples if they had read any books on sex. By the way, my practice was not to ask the premarital couples to share what was going on in their sexual relationship. I did not want to make them feel uncomfortable in the counseling process by getting too personal. Of course, I did spend a session with them talking about sex and giving them information about sex in marriage. I don't ask anymore whether premarital couples have read a book on sex. I already know the answer. None of them have. I encourage them to follow up on our counseling sessions by buying a Christian book on sex and reading it together. Sex in marriage is such an important part of marriage that it is worth doing some work in the sexual area. I even make some suggestions of some books that they can purchase. My wife and I have read several books on sex during our morning devotions. It is amazing how reading a book together can open the door to a meaningful discussion about sex. Do my wife and I have a perfect sexual relationship? No, we don't. Our sexual relationship is a work in progress. It will be that way our whole life long. Especially as you go through the stages of life, such as middle age, retirement, old age. Because we all are not perfect, all of us have some room for growth in our sexual relationship. God can help us grow toward His plan for fantastic sex in marriage. It is worth the work to have a great sexual relationship. Don't get stuck in unhealthy sexual patterns. Books on sex and podcasts on sex in marriage can be a great help. Just Google, "Christian books of sex in marriage." You will be surprised at the great many resources that will appear.

In my own marriage, there have been wonderful times of sex. There have also been some turbulent times. There have been times early in our marriage when I could not sleep in the same bed as my wife because the sexual feelings I was having were so strong that I could not sleep. My wife did not want to be sexual at those times. I did not want to force her into doing anything sexual that she did not want to do, so I went and slept in another room. Sometimes our sexual feelings can be very strong! Especially when we are young. Thankfully, those types of sleepless nights were not the norm for our marriage. It is not possible that a husband and wife will always have the same feelings about having sex. It is important that married couples talk about that difference, work it through, and stay committed to their marriage.

Years ago, when our children were young, my wife went away for a weekend on a retreat for women. That meant I had the responsibility for our four children from Friday afternoon until Sunday afternoon. That meant I had the pastoral responsibilities of Sunday morning without the help of my wife. By Sunday afternoon, I was ready for my wife to come home! I had been thinking about her all weekend. I wanted to connect with her when she came home. I wanted to be sexual with her when she came home. When she did come home, I caressed her and held her close to me. I told her I wanted to have sex with her. She chuckled at me. Better said, she laughed at me. I felt hurt. I felt belittled. I felt alone. I felt unloved. Maybe you have felt those same things in your marriage relationship. What did you do about them? Did you talk about them with your spouse? Did you deal with them in a way that strengthened the relationship? Or did you let the hurt you felt linger and fester?

My wife has also experienced emotional pain in our sexual relationship. There are times when our sexual relationship has been all about me. When that happens, she feels used. She does not feel loved. She feels hurt. There are times in a marriage sexual relationship that are frustrating. There are times when you feel like giving up on having sex with your spouse. There are times when you may feel angry about your sexual relationship. There are times when you feel hurt. I don't like those times. Neither do you. Becoming a new creation in Christ sexually means those times become less frequent or don't happen at all. Becoming a new creation in Christ means you do not let those difficult times ruin your relationship. Becoming a new creation in Christ sexually means you don't give up on trying to improve and grow your sexual relationship. You ask God to help you.

Since there are problems with sex in marriage, an important question must be asked. Why are there so many problems when it comes to sex in marriage? One of the reasons that there are sexual problems in marriage is that sex is the time when you are the most vulnerable with your partner. If you have problems in your relationship, those problems usually will show up in your sex life. It is difficult to be vulnerable with your partner sexually if you love them but do not like them. It is difficult to be vulnerable with your partner if you have been hurt in your relationship. If you have been hurt, you will subconsciously erect emotional walls to protect yourself. It is difficult to be vulnerable, open, or sexually free if you do not trust your partner. If sex is important to you, you will have sex frequently. If sex is a positive experience for you, you will want to have sex frequently. If you want to please God and be a new creation in Christ, you will work through the difficulties in your sexual relationship and strive to have a good sex life. It is very important to work toward having a good sexual relationship in marriage because it pleases God when you have a good sexual relationship in marriage. How do you do that?

Practice the sex trinity. By that, I mean there are three aspects about sex on which to focus, and these three aspects are not practical things like sexual positions, perfume, candles, romantic music, seductive dress, and other practical things. They are more important than these practical things. Now, sexual positions, perfume, candles, romantic music, seductive dress may enhance the sexual experience. But your attitude about your partner, marriage, sex, and God are more important. If you are married, I encourage you to invite God into your bedroom. That sounds like a threesome! And it is! A holy threesome. For some people, inviting God into the bedroom will be a new thing. Inviting God into the bedroom means you let God take over. You say to God that you want to be the best lover you can be, and you let God teach you how to be the best lover you can be. After all, God created sex, so He knows how it should work. God wants to grow you in the sex trinity. There are three key factors for better sex. These three things can only be practiced in your sexual relationship with your spouse by the work of God. Only God can work these three things in our hearts. Ready for this? What is the sex trinity?

The sex trinity:

1. Servant sex. The goal of pleasuring.
2. Grace sex. Remove the fear of rejection.
3. Worship sex. No idolatrous sex.

Number 1: *Servant sex.*

Sex in marriage means that each partner takes the role of being a servant of their spouse. Servants attend to the needs of others. Servants give of themselves. Servants serve. Jesus Himself said that He did not come to be served, but to serve (Mark 10:45). It is not always easy to be a servant. Why? Because we are basically self-centered. We want to be served! Husbands are like Christ when they approach sex not to be served but to serve. Wives are like Christ when they approach sex not to be served but to serve. Servants meet the needs of others. How do you know what your partner needs? You learn to perceive it through body language, and you learn it by your spouse telling you what they need. Sometimes the need of a wife is to be held, talked to, cared for, valued, and treated tenderly, without the focus being on orgasm. Other times the wife needs to be taken on a journey. The journey is to orgasm. This journey means the husband has to be patient, set his needs aside for a bit, and focus on pleasing his wife. Women need to be pleasured physically in order for their bodies to respond sexually. Most women need to be manually stimulated if they are to reach orgasm. This need puts the husband in the role of a servant. Sometimes the wife's role is simply to please her husband. This puts her in the role of a servant. Obviously, when both are being served by their spouse, there is a give and take. If either partner is only thinking of himself/herself, the sexual relationship will suffer. When both husband and wife give of themselves to pleasing their spouse, great things can happen. It takes time to be a servant. It takes personal sacrifice. It requires patience. It is part of being a new creation in Christ sexually.

When a balance of sexual fulfillment between a husband and a wife can be achieved, there is servant sex. Sometimes a husband will give himself to his wife to fulfill her sexually even though he does not achieve an orgasm. Sometimes a wife will give of herself to her husband to fulfill his sexual needs even though she does not achieve orgasm. That is servant sex. A woman's sexual response is much more complicated than a man's. The woman needs to be pleasured in order to respond sexually. That means she needs to be touched in a tender, loving way for a period of time. She has to relax and enjoy the pleasuring of her emotions and her body in order for her body to respond sexually. Pleasuring takes time. If the husband just wants to get down to business and get his needs met, he will not give the time and attention to being a servant to his wife. Men, let me say, it takes patience to be a good sexual partner. All your instincts may be pushing you to your sexual fulfillment. But what about your wife? In servant sex, you make the needs of your partner more important than your own needs. I have not always been good at servant sex. My guess is, most men would say the same thing. But you can get better at servant sex. You do that as you become a new creation in Christ sexually.

An older woman was reflecting with me and my wife about her different marriages. She had been married three times. All three husbands had died. She said that one of the men had some physical problems that made it difficult for him to have orgasms. He told her that he had made peace with that and that his goal was to receive pleasure when she received pleasure. He was okay with infrequent orgasms for himself but wanted to give of himself so that she could be pleasured. That is servant sex. Some women do not always want to have an orgasm. This happens for various reasons. She may be tired from the cares of the day. She may not be able or willing to expend the emotional energy needed for her body to respond. She may not trust that her husband will take the time to pleasure her. It is okay for the wife to not want to have an orgasm. Just be careful that it does not become the norm in your sexual relationship! When a wife does not have a desire for orgasm, she practices servant sex when she gives of herself to please her husband. And sometimes, this pleasing of one's spouse in servant sex is all that is needed for sexual fulfillment. There can still be pleasurable feelings when being held by your spouse, being loved by them, being touched, kissed, needed, even when there is no orgasm. The goal in the sexual experience is the sharing of love, and that need is different at different times for each partner in the relationship. The sharing of love is accomplished through servant sex. In servant sex, the goal is to please your partner. How well are you doing at being a servant of your spouse sexually

Number 2: *Grace sex.*

Grace is an interesting word. But I bet you never thought about grace being part of sex in marriage! Grace simply means that God has given us His undeserved favor. It means that God does not reject us. Even though we deserve for Him to reject us because we sin before Him, He does not reject us. Grace means that God continually reaches out to us with love and acceptance. Grace is unconditional love. Grace says, I love you no matter what. In fact, the Bible says that Jesus is called grace. "When the grace of God appeared..." (Titus 2:11) That passage is talking about Jesus. And didn't Jesus give grace to people when He walked on this earth? You bet. To a woman at a well in Samaria, who had been married five times and was living with a man, Jesus gave grace. To Peter, after he denied Jesus three times by a fireside, Jesus gave grace. Grace doesn't quit. When I see people who are having problems in their sexual relationship, it is often because one or both of them have quit trying. Grace does not quit.

Why is grace so important when it comes to sex in marriage? In order for the sexual relationship to be good, there must be the absence of the feeling of rejection. If you feel rejected by your partner, you will instinctively put up emotional walls between you and your partner for protection from hurt. You will do it subconsciously. Often you won't even realize you are doing it. Since sex is about intimacy and connection, you will not be able to connect emotionally or physically if there is a fear of being hurt or rejected by your partner.

It is easy to reject your marriage partner because they have not done what is loving. We can take hurtful things our partner has done during the day and carry that over to our sexual relationship. Grace changes that progression. Grace enables us to accept our partners, even if they have sinned. Love covers a multitude of sins (1 Peter 4:8). We all sin. You did not marry a perfect partner. You are not a perfect partner. The tendency is to let these imperfections get in the way of sexual intimacy. By grace, you set these imperfections aside. Love keeps no record of wrongs (1 Corinthians 13:5). Grace sex means you do not give up on trying to work on your sexual relationship. You treat your partner with unconditional love, just as you did when you first met him/her before you became aware of all his/her imperfections! You see the best in your partner. You work at being vulnerable with your partner. You work at trusting them with your deepest feelings. You do not let anxiety, fear, or apprehension become part of your sexual relationship. This can only happen by the grace of God.

Listen. If you are not practicing grace sex, you will hold back a part of yourself from your partner. Let me illustrate it this way. If you approach sex with only 25 percent of yourself, the part of yourself that you are willing to risk in the relationship, you will be guarding and withholding 75 percent of yourself from your partner. Do you want to settle for 25 percent sex, or go for 100 percent sex? The only way to give all of yourself to your partner and to accept all of your partner is by grace. That is grace sex.

Number 3: *Worship sex.*

Let me explain. I do not mean that you worship sex! What I mean is that you reserve your sexual relationship, in thought, and in actions, only for your partner. One thing that ticked God off in the Old Testament was when His people practiced idolatry. They went after other gods. In the commandments listed in Deuteronomy 5 and Exodus 20, God stated His desires for His people with these words, "Have no other gods before me." In the New Testament, Jesus told Satan that we are to worship the Lord and Him only (Matthew 4:10). God wants our single-minded devotion to Him and Him only. We are not to let anyone or anything get between us and God. The same is true in our sexual relationship with our spouse. That is what I mean by worship sex. No relational idolatry. No sexual idolatry. Our affections are to be for our spouse alone. That means no affairs, even emotional affairs.

I am not advocating that you treat your spouse as a God. That would be idolatry. I am saying that you look nowhere else for your sexual pleasure. You make a commitment to your spouse, and you keep it, whether sex in your life is poor or great, whether you are sick or healthy, rich with passion or impoverished, in the best or the worst, till death do you part. You can see how this kind of commitment relates to being a new creation in Christ. Christ is committed to us. He does not give up on us. He wants our wholehearted allegiance. Your spouse wants the same from you. And you want it from them.

This means, guys, that you don't look at other women. It is one thing to notice a beautiful woman. I don't believe we guys can stop noticing a beautiful woman. But we can stop what we think about when we see a beautiful woman. If you think something about that woman that, if you did it, it would be wrong before God, then the thought is wrong. If you stare at another woman, you are probably going somewhere in your mind that is not right. And your spouse, if they are with you, will notice it, if not feel it. That is sexual idolatry.

What if your spouse has had an affair? I have counseled many people where this has happened. Although sexual infidelity is a biblical reason for divorce (Matthew 5:31-32), it does not have to be so. If the offending partner is repentant and willing to completely break off the affair, and if the non-offending spouse is willing to forgive, then the relationship can be mended. If an affair has happened in your relationship, be sure to get some Godly counsel. A good counselor can help you work through the pain and rejection of an affair. A good counselor can help you understand why the offending partner thought an affair was an acceptable thing to do.

If the post affair relationship has any hope of healing and restoration, there has to be some kind of commitment to the former relationship. The reality is that with an affair, the offended partner has no real way to trust that their partner has ended the affair and is now willing to re-commit to their marriage. How will the innocent partner know the affair is over? Drastic measures need to be taken to build trust that the affair is over. I have even had some people call the person they have had an affair with, in my office, on the phone with their partner present, and have them tell the person they had an affair with that they no longer want to have any contact with them in any way. This does a great deal to begin to build trust back into the relationship. Every situation is different, and there are no pat answers. That is why it is essential to get professional counsel.

It takes intentional work to have a good sexual relationship. My wife and I had four children. When the children were young, we had to be creative to work on our sexual relationship. At times, we would lock the doors to the bedroom so that we did not fear the children would interrupt our intimate time. At times, we would take a nap during the day so that we could play together at night. That is what I call a ministry nap! Sometimes, we would get up early in the morning, before the children woke up so that we could connect sexually. Sometimes, we asked someone to take care of the children so that we could get away by ourselves and work on our sexual relationship. Notice I have used the word "work" a few times. We often do not see that there is some work to be done if we want to have a good sexual relationship. We want sex in marriage to simply be a spontaneous thing that happens naturally. Wrong! Most of the time, sex takes planning, talking, and work to make it a priority for the relationship. We have been created by God to have a sexual part of our life. If you have lost that sexual, loving feeling with your spouse, you can get it back. God wants to help you to do that.

I did not want this chapter to be an extensive treatise about sex in marriage. Many other people have written books on that subject. Check them out. Check out the website, "Authentic Intimacy," or the podcast "Java with Julie." Julie Slattery believes she has been called by God to help people recover a Biblical practice of sexuality. She has many podcasts that can be helpful in sexual relationship. Try to make your sexual relationship fresh, exciting, a new thing by being a new creation in Christ. Practice the sex trinity. How would you rate your sexual relationship in the three sex aspects I have discussed? Rate them on a scale of one to ten, one being poor, and ten being great.

1. Servant sex–1————————————————10

2. Grace sex–1————————————————10

3. Worship sex–1————————————————10

4. How much hurt are you experiencing in your sexual relationship?

5. What have you done to improve your sexual relationship?

CHAPTER EIGHT

Becoming a New Creation Verbally

One word can change everything. When a political election is held, and the votes are counted, the result can be summed up in a word. A candidate is either a loser or a winner. One word makes the difference. When a person has been battling cancer and has received a battery of chemo treatments, they may have an appointment with a doctor to hear about the results of the treatments. They may hear the word terminal, or remission. One word can make a difference. When someone is on trial for a crime and the jury finishes their deliberation, the verdict is handed to the judge and read to the people gathered in the courtroom. The judge will say either guilty or not guilty. One word can make a big difference. Do not underestimate the power of your words.

In each profession, there are different tools for each trade. A plumber will have certain tools he uses in his work. An electrician will have specific tools he uses in his work. An auto mechanic has specific tools he uses in his work. A mason has specific tools he uses in his work. My wife has specific tools she uses for sewing. My wife also likes to purchase specific tools to use when cooking.

A pastor uses the tool of words. Preaching and teaching involve the use of words. Words can convey the truth. Words can convict the heart and bring about repentance. Words can free a person from sin and death. Words can build up faith or tear down faith. Words can encourage a person or discourage a person. In your life, whether on the job, in a marriage, raising children, being a friend, or meeting a stranger, your words can have a profound impact on others. It is important that we develop the skill of using thoughtful, measured, crafted words.

You have probably heard it said that it is not so much what you say, but how you say it. So true. It takes time and work to craft our thoughts and feelings into words. Like any skill, this crafting of our thoughts into words can be learned and developed. Frankly, many people either don't share what they think and feel in words, or they don't spend the time and energy to develop the skill of using words. That is sad. Words are the way we define ourselves. Words are the way we connect with other people. What we say in any situation is very powerful. Becoming a new creation in Christ means we take the matter of crafting our words very seriously. We realize God can use our words to change our own lives and the lives of others. We realize we need God's help to become better at using words.

Words are powerful. Words can build up a person or tear down a person. Words can create. Words can create hope for the hopeless. Words can create courage in the fearful. Words can create vision. Words can create forgiveness where there is hurt. Words can create love for the unloved. Words can create inspiration for those who are stuck in a problem. Words can create things in the lives of other people. God created the universe, in the very beginning, with His Word. He said, "Let there be...and it was so" (Genesis 1:6-15). Jesus often did amazing things just by speaking a word. When Jesus cast out demons, He spoke a word. When Jesus healed people, He often spoke a word. When Jesus raised His friend Lazarus from the dead, He spoke a word. Jesus said, "Lazarus, come forth" (John 11:43-44). And Lazarus walked out of the tomb! Jesus' words were powerful! And our words are powerful!

How many of us have had people speak a word to us that profoundly affected the course of our life? I would say, all of us. At the age of eleven, I became a Boy Scout. I became an Eagle Scout, the highest rank in the Boy Scouts, at the age of fourteen. Both of my brothers are Eagle Scouts. Three Eagle Scouts in one family is not very common. When I was thirteen years old, one of the Boy Scout leaders said to me, "You have a lot of leadership qualities. Because of your leadership ability, I want you to be a troop leader." In those words, I was given affirmation. I was empowered. If God can create with a word, we become more like God when we create things in people by speaking a word to them. That is what it means to become a new creation in Christ verbally. We speak words of affirmation and life to people. This is a skill that anyone can learn if they are willing to follow the prompting of the Holy Spirit.

In the Lutheran Church-Missouri Synod, the church where I grew up and where I served as a pastor, we have the rite of Confirmation. Confirmation is typically not where you become a Christian. It is where you grow in the teachings of the Church and grow in your Christian faith. In the church that I grew up in, the confirmation instruction consisted of a two-year process for young people who were in the 7th and 8th grades. The classes took place on Saturday morning, starting at nine. It was during that time that, at the encouragement of my older brother, I decided to achieve the Boy Scout religious award, "God and Country." This meant that I would do homework on different areas of life and how the Christian faith affected those areas. There were different sections on the family, community, church, and friends. I would meet with my mentor, Rev. Otto Diefenbach, on a regular basis to discuss my answers in each of these areas of life. One time Pastor Diefenbach said to me, "Russ, you have a keen understanding of spiritual things, unlike many young people your age. You may want to think about being a pastor." That was all he said. But it planted a seed. A word was given. And that word stuck in my heart and mind. Words are powerful! I do think that God had already planted the seed, or word, in my heart to be a pastor. Pastor Diefenbach just confirmed it!

You never know how God will use a word that you say to others to profoundly affect their lives. I have had people come to me and say that I said something in a sermon that changed their life. They will say, "Do you remember when you said.....?" Often, I don't remember. But they have told me that the word I spoke changed their life.

When my daughter, my youngest child, was accepted into a PhD program in Biochemistry, she told me that she was not sure that she could do it, that she was not sure she had the ability to do it. My word to her was, "You have the ability. The question is whether you are willing to pay the price." I know she knew I knew something about paying the price for an education. Paying the price is not about paying the fees for credits. Paying the price means that you will study when you want to play. Paying the price means you may lose some sleep because you have to work on some class project into the night. I learned Latin, Greek, and Hebrew in college. I went to seminary for four years. I completed a PhD degree in Christian Counseling. She knew I had paid the price to achieve advanced degrees in college. Today, she is well on her way to completing her degree. She is paying the price. Words are powerful.

Words also have the power to wound, damage, or discourage. A father may say to a young adolescent, "You will never amount to anything." Translation: You don't measure up. You are substandard. You are defective. You are a loser. These words can be damaging. The young person may feel they should not even try to achieve something in his/her life if they are a loser. Or they may feel they need to achieve something great in their life to prove to their father that they are not a loser. Both paths are not healthy. Words are powerful.

A mother may have said to her young daughter when she could not find things in the home, "You have no common sense." Translation: You are stupid, intellectually challenged, defective. Ouch. When this young lady grows up, she may become very sensitive to things people say to her that make her feel like she is not very smart, when in reality, she may be very gifted in her ability to understand things in life. Words are powerful.

My father never told me he was proud of me. I knew he was proud of me, he just never said it. As a child, when I would go to bed, I would tell my father good night and that I loved him. He would say, "Good night, love you." I yearned for that affirmation from my father. My father was abusive. Often, during dinner, someone would end up crying because of something my father did. My mother would ask him to stop doing what he was doing. He would say to her, "You shut up, or you are next." He said this in front of me and my siblings. I heard it multiple times. My dad was threatening my mother in front of me. I did not like that. Even though both my parents have now died, I still deal with emotional pain about how my father treated my mother. I never saw my father being physically abusive to my mother. I don't think he ever abused her physically. Some of you reading this have seen physical abuse in your family. I am grieving with you about that. A man, if he is a real man, never physically abuses a woman, and he does not threaten to abuse a woman. The man that abuses a woman or threatens a woman is a wimp. He is so insecure within himself that the way he feels better about himself is to exert power over those who are less powerful. He is a wimp because he is so insecure. He is a wimp because he treats the weaker person poorly so that he can feel better about himself. Abusive people injure others. They don't care that they injure others. Words can injure others. The injury from hurtful or threatening words that are spoken can impact a person for the rest of their life. Words are powerful.

I think I have made the point that words are powerful, for good and for bad. So, how do we get better with words? How do we become a new creation in Christ verbally? If Jesus was good at words, and He was, He can help us do better with our words.

Let me suggest four things to work on verbally. They are not easy. They can only be done by the power of God and the leading of the Holy Spirit. These four skills are crucial to being a new creation in Christ verbally. Notice all four things I am suggesting begin with the letter D. Here they are:

1. Develop the skill of using words.
2. Discover words that build others up.
3. Determine to speak the truth in love.
4. Discern what is good humor and what is bad humor.

Number 1: *Develop the skill of using words.*

Any skill can be learned. When my boys were in t-ball, they were afraid to be at-bat. After all, there is a ball being thrown at you! But as they grew in the skill of hitting the ball, they were no longer afraid to be at-bat. If you ask a baseball player what is his/her favorite position on the field to be playing, he will say, to be at-bat! That is where the action is. They have learned the skill of batting. You can learn the skill of using words.

One of my seminary professors encouraged us who were studying to be pastors to read the dictionary. I thought, *You must be crazy!* Who sits down and reads a dictionary? That seminary professor knew that being a public speaker, and being a pastor, involved mastery of words. You can grow in the skill of using words if you increase your vocabulary! Go, Webster! The skill that is needed to become a new creation in Christ is to identify the thoughts and feelings that you have and to put them into words. It is like painting a picture. When you paint a picture, you take a landscape, some sort of real-life situation, or maybe an imaginary situation, and you put it on the canvas so that everyone can see it. You take the abstract and make it real. Using words is a process just like that. You take a thought and frame it with words. You take your feelings and frame them with words. You can paint a word picture with the words you speak.

If I say, "That person is as cold as an iceberg." I am painting a verbal picture. What I mean is, the cold person seems void of feelings. They are unmoved, hard of heart, even dangerous to be around! If I say, "He is strong as an ox." What image comes to your mind? Jesus did this many times in the Bible. He said, "I am the vine, and you are the branches" (John 15). Once He described that word picture, He could elaborate on it with things like bearing fruit or being pruned. When you tell someone a story about something in your life, you are drawing a word picture. You are describing something to someone that you experienced so that person can join you in the experience. Your story would include facts, feelings, sounds, and things that you saw. You are telling the story so that someone can connect with what you experienced. You paint a word picture for them. This is a skill that anyone can develop.

Years ago, my wife told me she wanted to paint a word picture for me. I thought, This will be exciting! Not! She asked me to think about a scene in the forest. Going through the forest was a train track. You can hear in the distance a train coming down the track. Smoke is billowing from the train stack. The train is moving fast. The train is coming around a bend in the distance. A woman is tied to the train track, in the path of the coming train. Just then, a uniformed officer rides up on a big horse. My wife asked me what this picture she was painting meant. She told me she was the woman tied to the train track. I asked her if I was the hero coming to rescue her? She said, "No. You are the train." I got the point. That, my friends, is a word picture. Needless to say, I put the brakes on the train. I stopped the train and put on the uniform of the officer! True story. That is a word picture.

One time I had a counseling session with a young man. This young man had very low self-esteem. He did not think he could accomplish anything. He would not even try to accomplish anything. He had a fear that if he tried to do something, he might fail. His parents tried to motivate him to try some new things. He would not do it. His teacher tried to help him accomplish some tasks. He would not even try to do what she said. I decided to paint a word picture for him. I asked him if he had ever heard the story of the little train that could. He said he had not read that story. I told him about this little train that stopped moving before a big mountain. The train looked at the mountain and thought that he could never go over that mountain. The train was stuck on the track, just looking at the big mountain. Then the train began to say to himself over and over, "I think I can, I think I can." Then he started to climb the mountain. It was tough for this little train to climb the mountain, but he kept saying to himself, "I think I can, I think I can." And know what? He climbed that mountain. I told him he was like that train. He could look at the mountains in his life and think, *I will never climb this mountain.* Or he could say, "I think I can." I asked him to be like the little train that could. He started to go up the mountains in his life. That is the power of a word picture.

Some people are verbally lazy. They just won't work on forming their words. Forgive me for saying it, but I have seen it all too often: men are often lousy at framing their words. Their wife may come to them with a great deal of emotion and want them to talk. Because of all the emotions brought by the wife and brought on within the husband, the husband's feelings are so confused and jumbled up that they don't know how to say what they are feeling and are afraid of getting in trouble if they do talk. The result? They give silent treatment. They shut down. They refuse to feel. Getting silent feels safe. But being silent hurts relationships. What I encourage men and women to do when they feel overwhelmed in a situation is to ask for a time out. To simply say, "What you are saying is very important to me. I don't know how to respond right now. I need a little time to work on it, to sift through my thoughts, and how I will share those thoughts with you." This works a lot better than the silent treatment! When I did this with my wife years ago, she responded, "How much time?" Fair question. She was giving a trust statement. She was saying, "Can I trust you to actually work on this and come back to me and talk about this?" She wanted a specific time when I would be prepared to talk. I gave her a specific time. And you know what? When the agreed-upon time came later that night, she came up to me and said that it is time to talk. And I did. Because I had worked on sifting through my thoughts and framing my words.

A couple contacted me for marriage counseling some years ago. I met with the wife, by herself, first. She told me she was emotionally starving in the relationship. She said that her husband rarely, if ever, talked with her. He typically would come home from work and watch TV until he went to bed. She described her relationship with her husband like a hot, dry, arid desert, where nothing can grow and the ground is cracked and hard. She was surely using some words! She painted a word picture about her relationship with her husband.

A few days later, I met with her husband, by himself. I told him what she had said. I told him that if he did not make some changes, his marriage would likely end. He told me he loved his wife. He wanted to work on the marriage. I told him he had to develop the skill of sharing his thoughts and feelings with his wife. If he would not work on this skill, I told him I did not have much hope his marriage would last. I told him that sharing his thoughts and feelings is not that difficult. I challenged him. I said, "When you come home at the end of the day from work, be prepared to share the best part of your day and the worst part of your day. Every day there is surely a good part and a bad part. There were things that were difficult for you, and there were things that made you feel good." I gave him some examples. I told him, "On your lunch break, spend some time thinking about the best part of your day and the worst part of your day. Jot down your thoughts on a piece of paper. On your way home from work, look at what you wrote on that piece of paper. When you walk in the door to your house, go find your wife. Tell her what was good about your day and what was the most difficult part of your day." I asked him if he was willing to do this. He said he would.

The next appointment was to be with the couple together. They came into my office holding hands, laughing, and google-eyeing one another. After they sat down, I asked them what happened since I had last met with them? The woman said she did not know what I had done to her husband, but he was a different man. She said that they had some really good talks. She said she could not be happier with their marriage. That was the first and the last time I met with them. That husband was on his way to becoming a new creation in Christ verbally.

There are basically five different feeling areas and numerous expressions of our feelings in each area. Decide which area expresses where you are in your feelings and why. Figure out what words you will use and how you will share your feelings. I tell people in the marriage seminars I have led and in counseling sessions, "You cannot love someone you do not understand, and you cannot understand your partner unless they share themselves with you." So simple. So difficult. But it can be learned.

The five basic areas of feelings include being glad, being sad, being mad, having desires, and meeting needs. In each of these areas, there are many ways our feelings can manifest themselves in our lives. Land on one of those feeling areas. Explore it. Expand it. Examine it. Then express it. When we were camping with some friends, my friend and I decided to play Disc golf. I wanted my wife to go and play with us. I was expressing a desire to her. I told her I had a need to get some exercise and to spend some time with her. She said she would play Disc golf with us. I told her that made me happy because it would be an experience we could share. When I threw a bad shot into the woods, it made me sad. I told my wife I did not like that shot! When she threw a shot and hit me in the head, that made me mad. I said, "Thanks a lot, dear!" Then we laughed about the whole experience. See how easy it is to state your feelings?

When you state your thoughts and feelings, you are saying to the world and to those you care about, "I am. I exist. I am a person. This is who I am." Then they know who you are and can begin to connect with how you have defined yourself and deal with it. As you think about developing the skill of using words, are you verbally challenged? Becoming a new creation in Christ means you develop the skill of using words to define what you think and how you feel to others in your life. The more you work on this skill, the easier it becomes to share yourself with others.

Number 2: *Discover words that build others up.*

Once we recognize that our words can build up a person or tear them down, it is our task as new creations in Christ to determine how to speak words that build others up. Sounds so simple, but it is a skill that needs to be learned. In Ephesians 4:24, we are instructed, "Do not let any unwholesome talk come out of your mouth, but only what is helpful for building others up." Notice the word "any" is used. Unwholesome talk belittles other people. Unwholesome talk unfairly criticizes others. Unwholesome talk hurts the feelings of others. To not let any unwholesome words come out of our mouth is a tall order! You build up others when you give them words of affirmation and validation and want to make them feel good about themselves.

You build others up when you encourage them to live by faith in God. You build others up when you affirm their worth. You build others up when you do not respond to ugly words with ugly words. Instead, you respond to ugly words with kind words. Not easy to do. But part of becoming a new creation in Christ verbally.

It is vital when wanting to build others up that you do not allow others to control your thoughts, your feelings, or your words. Own your own thoughts. Own your own feelings. Do not blame your thoughts and feelings on the behavior of another person. Own your own words. Don't respond to harsh comments with harsh comments. Don't respond to anger with anger. Own your feelings and make a choice about them. Choose to use words that build others up and don't tear them down.

It is amazing how a situation can come up that will challenge whether we use our words to build others up or tear them down. Often the first thought we have about what we can say is not the best thing to say. Our initial feelings can be motivated by our sinful nature. Becoming a new creation in Christ means we develop the skill of making decisions about how we will respond verbally. This is a skill that can be developed.

A few months ago, my wife and I went camping in Key Largo, Florida. We had decided to get up early and go fishing in a blow-up kayak. With what I know now, I would not recommend going fishing in a blow-up kayak. Inflatable kayaks are not very stable. Inflatable kayaks do not respond favorably to fish hooks, rocks, or branches! At 6 a.m., I went to a bait shop to purchase some live shrimp. When I parked my car at the bait shop, my car was the only car in the parking lot. When I came out of the bait shop, there was another car in the parking lot. A man was walking into the bait shop as I was coming out. He said, "You took two parking spaces. You retard." Now I had a decision. I could respond to his comment with a declaration of my educational achievements. I could respond with a put-down to him. I could respond with a clear explanation of the parking lot situation. There were over twenty parking spaces in the parking lot. The spaces were not clearly marked. Besides, it was still dark! But I had a choice. I said to him, "It is really a nice morning. Have a great day!" The point is, we can rise above the perceived put-down and take the high road. We can choose to not let any unwholesome words come out of our mouths and to build others up. It is not always easy. Do I respond with kindness all the time when someone has been unkind to me? Not all the time. I won't give you any examples of how I have responded poorly to other people! But I have! The point is, we need God's help, by the Holy Spirit, to consistently speak words that build others up rather than to tear others down. We need to grow in becoming new creations in Christ in order to speak what is helpful rather than what is hurtful.

We can build others up by giving them affirmation about something they have done in the past. We can commend them on a job well done. This means saying things like, "You did a great job. I was really blessed by how you handled that task. I appreciate what you have done." Usually, what we do is speak about a person's past behavior in a negative way. If you are thinking of something another person has done in the past that was wrong or sinful, you will speak to their past failures and criticize them for their failures. Have you ever wondered why, when you have done this, the person you are speaking to gets defensive and upset at your comments? People usually know when they have made a mistake. Hindsight is 20/20. We can look at the past and see what we did and realize pretty easily that what we did was not right, correct, or wise. It does not build others up when we constantly correct them. Be careful about how often you speak about a person's failures. Instead, look to the future. Looking to the future says to someone, "I believe in you."

When the apostle Peter denied Jesus three times at the fireside outside Pilate's judgment hall, Jesus knew what Peter had done. After the resurrection, Jesus spoke to Peter with a future orientation. Jesus said, "Simon, (Peter), do you love me?" Jesus told Peter to feed His sheep. In other words, "Peter, you have a job to do. There are people who need you to speak the truth to them. Don't get stuck in the past." Jesus reinstated Peter. He did not condemn him. Jesus told Peter that He still believed in him and that He had work for Peter to do. He said, "Feed my sheep" (John 21:15-17). Jesus, who was the Son of God, had a vision for the life of Peter. God has a vision for our lives as well. That means God has a future orientation for our lives. We become new creations in Christ when we speak words to people that show we believe in them no matter what they have done, that God has a plan for their lives, a plan that will accomplish good things. That evidences a future orientation in our thinking and in our words.

Number 3: *Determine to speak the truth in love.*

The Bible in Ephesians 4:15 encourages us to speak the truth in love. Again, it is not easy to speak the truth in love consistently. Speaking the truth in love can only be done by the guidance of the Holy Spirit. When Jesus met a woman at the well in Samaria in John, Chapter 4, He did not say to her, "You are a miserable failure. You have made a wreck of your life. You have been married five times, and you are living with a man right now. The law of God says you should be stoned (put to death)." That might have been the truth, but it was not a word that would have been spoken in love. Instead, Jesus reached out to her in love. His words to her in effect said, "You are hurting and have tried to find love in your life but have come up empty. I want to help you with that. I want to help you with your deepest need, to be loved. I want to give you living water, the water of my love that will meet your need for love so that you never feel unloved again." Wow! That is speaking the truth in love.

When Jesus told His disciples that He would be handed over to the teachers of the law, be killed, but on the third-day rise, Peter said to Jesus, "Lord, this will never happen to you!" Jesus spoke the truth in love. He said to Peter, "Get behind me Satan. You do not have in mind the things of God but the things of men" (Matthew 16:13-23). Now, Jesus is the Son of God, and God is love, so we must hear these words of Jesus to Peter as speaking the truth in love. What was Jesus really saying? Jesus was saying, "Peter, you are in a spiritual battle. I care so much about you that I want you to win this battle. Evaluate where your feelings are coming from. Are your feelings based on the truth of who I am and why I have come? Or are they based on your desire to fight and win and flash a sword as you will do in the garden of Gethsemane when I am arrested? Peter, what is your motivation? Peter, Satan is after you. Don't let him win the day." That is speaking the truth in love!

Will you struggle with me about what it means to speak the truth in love? Many people think that if they say what is on their mind, they are speaking the truth in love. That is not necessarily true. It is rarely true. You can blast someone with emotional criticism and belittle them even when you are thinking that you care about them. That is not speaking the truth in love. You can be silent when someone is going the wrong way. You may know that if they keep going that way, they will make a wreck of their life. You may decide to be silent because you think they may not like to hear the truth. That is not speaking the truth in love. Sometimes speaking the truth in love involves saying the difficult thing to someone who is hurting themselves and others, but speaking to them in a loving, encouraging way.

I know a man who worked at Kennedy Space Center in a high-level capacity. He was a very gifted man. He had helped the church in many ways with his ability to oversee building projects. But he was abrasive when it came to his relationship with others in the church. At one point, I asked him to come into my office for a chat. Kind of like going to the principal's office when you are in school! I spoke the truth in love. I told him that he was a great asset to the church. I told him I appreciated all that he had done for the church. But there was one aspect I asked him to work on. I said, "You are often adversarial in the way that you deal with other people. This is not the way

Christ wants us to behave. I would like to ask that you work at being more congenial. We are all working for the same goal in the church. Our goal is to support the work of God and the work of the church. Other church members are not the enemy. Will you try to get along better with other people?" He said that he would. And he did. That is speaking the truth in love. It is difficult to speak the truth in love. Sometimes we speak the truth in love to someone, but the person we are speaking to will not receive what we are saying. Speak the truth anyway, in love.

Several years ago, a man came to my office just before a Lenten service. Since it was the beginning of the church season of Lent, it was in the winter. Winter in Florida means the temperature at night might be between forty to fifty degrees. Pretty cold for us! I will call the man Frank. Obviously, not his real name. He was worn out. He was hungry. He had not been sleeping very well. He had been working as a diver in the construction of a bridge in our town. He was sleeping in a tent near the inter-coastal waterway, the Banana River. So, he had no permanent dwelling, no running water, no cooking facilities. He told me he was at the end of his rope. He did not know how much longer he could go on. He asked if I could help him. I found out that he was getting paid each Friday, would spend his paycheck on alcohol and drink through the weekend until he had to go back to work. At the end of the weekend, he had no money left from his paycheck. So, I spoke the truth in love to him. First, I told him to start coming to church, which he did. Next, I told him to bring his paycheck to me every Friday and leave 75 percent of it with me so that he could save some money and move toward more permanent housing. He agreed to give me part of his paycheck each Friday. Third, I asked him to meet with me on a weekly basis to talk about his drinking, which he agreed to do. Fourth, I asked him to start going to AA meetings at least once per week, which he agreed to do as well. I spoke the truth in love to him.

Did it work out great for Frank? Not hardly. He was able to eventually buy a trailer, and because of his handyman ability, he was able to fix up the old broken-down trailer that he had bought. He met a girl, and they moved in together. They had a child together. All during this time, I would meet with Frank and talk about how things were going. The interesting part was, however, when I did not see Frank for a period of time, I knew he had gone back to drinking. Every once in a while, he would show up at my office. He usually showed up at my office when he realized he had once again made a mess of his life. I would tell him that if he did not stop drinking, he would lose his girl, his son, and his trailer. That is exactly what happened. The police were frequent visitors to his trailer.

I spoke the truth in love to Frank, but Frank would not make the changes he needed to make to take control of his life. I met with him off and on for several years, trying to be a friend to him and to point him in a more healthy direction. The last time he came to see me, he came to the church on a bicycle. He had all his earthly possessions in a backpack. I am making this story short, so I am leaving out a great deal of detail. By his own admission, he told me that he was drinking 24/7. He was sleeping in a lawn chair on the beach. He was having signs of physical breakdown. I am leaving out discussions about detox, hospital admissions, AA meetings, and other ways he tried to better his life. The last time I spoke to him, I told him that if he did not stop his drinking, he would be dead, probably within the next few months. I told him it was his last chance to make a change and that I would still help him to do that. Frank did not stop drinking. Frank died from an accident two months after I last met with him. You can speak the truth in love to some people, and they will not receive what you are saying to them. Speak the truth in love anyway. Speaking the truth in love may make all the difference, so the risk of speaking the truth in love is worth it.

You see, our responsibility is to speak the truth in love. It is not our responsibility what people do with the truth we speak to them. Sometimes though, people hear what we say, recognize it as truth from God, and act on it. When God allows us to be involved in a situation like this, it is a great blessing. We are not the truth. God is the truth. Jesus said, "I am the way, the truth, and the life" (John 14:6). God is the truth. Sometimes, however, people will not listen to the truth, even if you speak the truth in love. Speak the truth anyway.

It is not always easy to speak the truth in love. A father came into my office to speak to me about his son. The father did not agree with the wedding of his son. The father did not think the woman his son was going to marry was a good choice. The wedding was to take place in a city in another state. The father had decided he would demonstrate his disagreement of the wedding by not attending the wedding. I asked the father if he thought that if he did not go to the wedding, his refusal to attend the wedding would stop his son from getting married to this girl. The father said his son would, regretfully, go through with the wedding service, with or without him being present. The father felt that he could not give his blessing to the service. He thought that his presence was, in effect, giving his blessing. I spoke the truth in love. I told him that it might not be a wise decision to not attend the wedding service. I told him to rethink his decision. I told him his daughter-in-law and his son would remember his decision to not attend the wedding as rejection from him for the rest of their lives. I asked him, "Is the statement you are making by not attending the wedding worth that?" Now, I could have said that you are proud, controlling, and angry, and you need to repent. Where would that have gone? He would have probably left my office and rejected me! But he listened to me and did what I recommended. He went to the wedding, and he gave the blessing of his presence. He told his son what he thought about the wedding, but he supported his son's decision even though he did not agree with him. He spoke the truth in love. I spoke the truth in love. Not always easy to do, but definitely the God way to go.

There are two extremes in speaking the truth in love. You can choose to not speak the truth in love; therefore, you will be silent when you need to speak. Or you will speak what may be true, but it is not perceived as being said in love, and therefore what you say only makes matters worse. On the one side, to be silent would be an attempt to avoid any kind of conflict. On the other side, there is the desire to criticize someone no matter what the consequences. Neither extreme is the way of love. There is a time to speak and a time to be silent. There is a time when it is best to be slow to speak, quick to listen, and slow to become angry (James 1:19). There is also a time to be angry and to speak in anger to others. Look at Jesus when He cleansed the temple. He did not say, "Hey you guys, you are getting off base. I don't think the temple is the place to have the smell of animals and the waste of animals. I don't think the temple is a place of commerce. Can I get a witness?" No. He turned over their tables and drove them from the temple, speaking the truth in love, "You are making my Father's house a den of thieves!" The zeal of God's house consumed Him (Matthew 21:12-13). There is a difference. When you speak the truth in love, you don't sugarcoat the problem. You confront the wrong with words of love. Yet, be careful that you don't go so far in trying to defend the righteousness of God that you end up wanting to call down fire from heaven to consume someone who is doing something you are not comfortable with. That is not speaking the truth in love. The point is, there are times when we speak the truth in love in a forceful way.

Probably the key to speaking the truth in love is to discern our motive in speaking. I believe it is always good when speaking to someone to ask ourselves what we want to accomplish by what we say. It is also important to filter our words through the fruit of the spirit. Am I speaking in love? Is what I am saying kind? Is what I am saying under self-control? Am I being meek? Am I being led by the Spirit or the sinful flesh? What is the goal I am seeking to accomplish? What is our motive when we talk to someone about something that is wrong or difficult?

To speak the truth in love means to speak God's truth, in God's way, in God's timing. We can only do that as we become new creations in Christ.

Number 4: *Discern what is good humor and what is bad humor.*

Just to say that there is good humor and bad humor is to acknowledge that there is a difference between good and bad humor. Obviously, bad humor is bad. Duh. Good humor is good. Bad humor puts someone down. Bad humor is hurtful to others. Bad humor mocks someone. Bad humor is filled with sarcasm. Bad humor is bad, bad, bad.

Good humor is good and even necessary. Humor is very helpful in getting us through a difficult time. Humor lightens a stressful situation. We have a plaque hanging in our house that says, "Angels fly because they take themselves lightly." LOL, I think Jesus snickered when He heard His disciples complain that the people who had been on a mountain side listening to Jesus speak all day needed to be sent away so that they could get something to eat. You can read about that in the Gospel of John, Chapter 6. Jesus said in response to His disciples, "You feed them." LOL, You feed them! Yeah right. It was not a put down of the disciples, nor an indictment of the people. Jesus already knew what He was going to do. To His disciples, He was saying, "You think you have a problem? You think I have a problem? Wait until you see what happens. You are about to have your socks blown off!" And what did Jesus do? He fed the whole crowd with a boy's lunch, and then He left the disciples, after the crowd was fed, each holding a basket full of food! Can you hear Jesus laughing when they came back to Him at the end of feeding that crowd with their baskets full of food?

I want to give you some examples of bad humor. If you watch late-night TV and catch the comedians, you will hear examples of bad humor. If you laugh at someone who fails, that is bad humor. When the show American Idol started airing, I was not happy watching it. In the early seasons of American Idol, the judges made fun of the sincere attempt of people to sing. They made fun of them wanting to be the next American Idol. I am sure the people who tried out signed a release that allowed the producers to air their performance. The show used some of the people who tried out to cater to the human desire to make fun of others and to make sport of them. That is bad humor. Instead of screening the singers to determine who could actually sing and who could not sing, they set them up to use them for entertainment. That made me angry. I was not entertained.

Early in my ministry, I served in a small church in a small town. In a small town, everyone knows one another. And they know everyone's business. The people in the church had known one another all of their lives. The men had a practice of making jokes about their wives. The men made sport of their wives. In a group of people, they would make condescending remarks about women and their wives. If one of the men asked another man what he had been doing, the response was, "I had to do women's work. I had to vacuum and wash the dishes." Another would say his wife asked him about how a new dress looked. He said, "It is not the dress that is the problem, it is what is in the dress." Another man would say he had eaten meatloaf that night, but he would follow that comment up with, "But I couldn't tell you what kind of meat it was." Another would say, "When she says it is time to get ready and go somewhere, I know that I have about two hours." All the men would laugh.

Yuk, yuk, yuk. The women would roll their eyes or stare at the floor and take the brunt of the jokes. That is bad humor. By the way, I spoke the truth in love to those men, and they began to curb those put-downs. Bad humor hurts. Period. It has no place in the speaking of the people of God. Period.

Good humor can take a bad situation and turn it around for good. Good humor recognizes that we are all human and make mistakes often. Good humor often pokes fun at ourselves without putting ourselves down or defining us as defective people. Good humor can make people feel good about themselves and about the fact that God loves them no matter what silly behaviors they display.

Let's explore good humor. Recently my wife and I went on a trip to Wisconsin to see our two oldest sons and their families. It was great to have some of our grandchildren stay with us in the camper! On one occasion, the GPS in my truck was directing us to a road that I did not want to take. I asked my wife to look up the route on the GPS on her phone. Her phone was directing us to take a different route. My wife asked, "Do you want me to tell you which roads to take?" I said she could do that only if she spoke to me like the nice woman on my truck GPS. So, she talked very kindly, saying, "In a quarter of a mile, turn right. Now proceed ten miles." She asked me why the truck GPS was always a woman speaking? I told her that is because men are used to having women tell them what to do. We both laughed at that. My response was kindhearted and true!

One Sunday, as I was preaching the message, a moth began flying in front of me, back and forth. I could see the people watching the moth. The heads of the people were turning back and forth as they watched the path of the moth. I realized at that moment, pretty smart guy, that the people were not listening to me, but watching the moth! So, without really thinking about what I was doing, I swiped my hand in front of me, and by the grace of God, I caught the moth in my hand. Now I had a dilemma. If I crushed the moth in my hand, all the women would gasp at the cruelty they were witnessing right before their eyes. I had the mean thought that I should kill the moth and gain victory over the obvious distraction. I was also afraid of the reaction I would receive if I committed murder right before the eyes of the people in the church. What should I do? What would I do? I said to the people that I would be back in a moment. I took the moth in hand to a nearby door and released the moth out the door into the wild. Then I went back to the pulpit. The people started laughing. Wanting to "spiritualize" the moment, I said, "Jesus taught, Blessed are the merciful!" More laughter. That is good humor. I have no idea how I finished that sermon. Briefly, I expect. That sermon has been known as the "moth message."

A few months ago, my second son, Philip, went fishing in a kayak. Let me paint the picture. His wife had their oldest child in her kayak, and Philip had his fishing pole and two of the younger children in his kayak, a single person kayak. The children were five and three years old. A recipe for disaster! Needless to say, in the course of events, he lost his fishing pole. He was probably more interested in trying to save his children than his fishing pole. At least he made the children more important than the fishing pole! I laughed with him, and we talked about how much more valuable children are than a fishing pole, hoping to ease the pain of his loss.

A couple of months later, my wife and I were in the Florida Keys fishing in a two-person kayak. It was an inflatable kayak. We had to go through a cut that was very narrow, with trees hanging down around us and obstacles in the way. I did not want to puncture the inflatable kayak, lest we lose everything and have to swim back to the dock. When we emerged from the brush a little way, I realized that I had lost my fishing pole. The fishing line had been in the water since I had been trolling for fish. Trolling for fish in an inflatable kayak. Let me tell you, it is hard to paddle, watch for obstacles, watch the bait bucket, protect my wife, and watch your pole at the same time. All of a sudden, I realized that I had lost my fishing pole. I had no idea when it slipped away. Probably a huge fish got on the line and pulled the pole out of the kayak! Not. When I told my son what had happened, I told him that we are both experts at "pole-be-gone" fishing. You want to lose a pole fishing? Call us. We will show you how it is done. Like son, like father. I told him that I did not want him to outdo me. If he could lose a pole, so could I! Want to go fishing with me in an inflatable kayak? No guarantee what will happen to your pole or how many fish you will catch! LOL.

Most Christian comedians are good at good humor. My wife and I watched a DVD by Christian comedian, Tim Hawkins. In one of the sets, he talked about hand raising in church. Some people are hand-raisers, and some people are not hand-raisers. He talked about different kinds of hand-raisers. Some people raise their hands like a TV antenna. Some people prefer the touch-down type of hand raising. Some people use the window washing hand raise. Some people do the rock-the-baby-type of hand gesture. The really creative hand-raisers pattern their hand-raising after The Village People–Y-M-C-A. I am sure God is really not that interested in what type of hand raiser you are. Tim Hawkins's comments about hand-raising were hilarious. It was good humor.

The Psalmist says that he will lift up his hands unto the Lord (Psalm 63:4). Often in the Old Testament and the New Testament, people prostrated themselves before the Lord when they worshiped (Nehemiah 8:6, Revelation 7:11). I guess we could say that according to Biblical worship patterns, people need to get prostrate in worship or take their shoes off like God told Moses to do in Exodus 3. Which, by the way, people in Ethiopia do when they enter a church! The point is that there are many ways to worship. It is okay to have fun with hand raising in worship. It may move us to evaluate why we raise our hands, and to accept various ways of hand raising. It is okay not to raise hands in worship. It is okay to find humor in ordinary things people do, as long as we are not being hurtful to others.

How are you doing in being a new creation in Christ verbally? Be honest. You may want to ask the people closest to you how you are doing to rate you. Rate the following aspects of being a new creation in Christ verbally. And have fun with it!

1. Develop the skill of using words. 1=low.............10=high
2. Discover words that build others up. 1=low.........10=high
3. Determine to speak the truth in love. 1=low.........10=high
4. Discern what is good humor and what is bad humor and only speak what is good humor! 1=low..............10=high

CHAPTER NINE

Becoming a New Creation in Your Generosity

Early in our marriage, I loaned a neighbor, a single mother, one of our cars so that she could go shopping. I thought to myself, *How generous you are!* When she brought the car back, I noticed that she had not filled up the gas tank, nor did she offer to give us any money for the use of the car. I thought, *No problem. At least she did not drive the car very much.* Then I noticed that there was water leaking from the front of the car. Upon further inspection, I saw that she had run into something, dented the bumper, and damaged the radiator. The water that was leaking was antifreeze from the damaged radiator. When I saw the damage that was done, I was angry. I was angry that she did not tell me about the damage or offer to pay for the damage. I had to walk around the yard for a while and cool down. I knew she did not have the money to fix the car. I had to buy a new radiator and fix the car myself. I left the bumper the way it was as a reminder to me to never let her borrow my car again! That is when God started working on me. This thought came to my mind. I believe it was a thought from God. God asked me, "Is the car your car or my car?" I had to admit that the car really belonged to God. God said, "If I decided to take the car away from you, can you live with that?" I decided that I could live with that. Then God said, "If she wants to borrow the car again, will you let her?" I told God that if she ever wanted to borrow the car again, I would drive her to where she needed to go. She never asked to borrow the car again. Generosity can be difficult!

Have you loaned something to someone, only to have to borrow it back? I have. Have you loaned something to someone and never saw what you loaned again? I have. Have you ever loaned someone some money and never gotten repaid? I have. Have you ever struggled with being generous? I have. Becoming a new creation in Christ means we grow in the practice of generosity.

God loves a cheerful giver (2 Corinthians 9:7). It is amazing to me that the disciples remembered the words of Jesus and recorded them in the book of Acts. Think about the words of Jesus recorded in Acts 20:35, "It is more blessed to give than to receive." These words are only recorded in the book of Acts, but they obviously were accepted by the early believers as the words of Jesus. Jesus must have said them often. It is more blessed to give than to receive. Sometimes it feels to me that it is more blessed to receive than to give! I don't know about you but living with the mindset that it is more blessed to give than to receive is not natural for me, nor is it easy. I struggle at times with being generous! I admit it! Do you? Sometimes God has to extract gifts from us! He has to pry our hands off our money. Generosity involves not only our money but our material goods, as well as our time.

God is abundantly generous. God gave us all we have. Ultimately, everything belongs to God. When you leave this earth, you take nothing with you. You leave it all here. God loans us everything we have to be used for His glory. God is generous in that He gave us His only begotten Son, Jesus Christ, to be our Savior. And finally, God wants to give us eternal life. God does not loan us our goods at interest. God does not make us sign a promissory note before he gives us things. God gives us everything free and clear. If you want to grow in being more like Christ, to be a new creation in Christ, you must grow in generosity. Our generous God wants us to grow in the joy of giving. It is amazing to me that some people who think they are generous, are not. Some people who think they are not generous, are. Some people who are very wealthy are not very generous. Some people who are not wealthy are very generous. Why is that? The answer is simple. Some wealthy people tend to find their security in their wealth. Wealthy people tend to think that they became wealthy because of hard work and sacrifice. Wealthy people tend to think that other people could achieve what they have achieved with hard work and sacrifice. Therefore, wealthy people tend to think that when someone is in need, they have been lazy, and they do not want to reward the laziness of those less fortunate. Most people who are not wealthy trust God will provide what they need. They have to trust God. So, it is easier for them to be generous because they live day by day, trusting God to provide. They know the truth of Jesus' words, "It is more blessed to give than to receive."

How can we grow in the spirit of generosity? To be truly generous, it is important to plan to be generous. That sounds so simple. It is not that simple. Generosity involves sacrifice. If a gift to someone does not cost me anything, then I have not really been that generous, have I? If we plan to limit our spending so that we not only have enough to give an offering for the support of God's kingdom, but also have set aside something to give to those in need, we have been intentional about being generous, and planned to be generous. Then, when we have the opportunity to be generous, we will not feel squeezed or in a pinch financially, for we planned in advance to be generous. How many people plan ahead to be generous? Not very many. Planning to be generous is part of what the Bible means when it says, "Grow in the grace of giving" (2 Corinthians 8:7). This does not mean we have to sell all we have and take on a life of voluntary poverty. If that were true, we would be in the position that we would need someone to be generous to us! It means that we plan to be generous so that we can regularly look for ways to practice the generosity we have already planned to do. And if we see people that really have a need, we go beyond what we have planned to do and stretch our faith that God will take care of us. It is a great joy to be a blessing to people in need. God loves a cheerful giver (2 Corinthians 9:7). There is great joy and great blessing in being generous.

Nearly twenty years ago, someone in our church gave my wife and me a fully-funded trip to Ethiopia. How generous of that couple! They had been all over the world and decided that Ethiopia was as close to experiencing life at the time of Jesus as anywhere they had been. They were not talking about the big cities, like the capital city of Ethiopia, Addis Ababa. They were talking about the undeveloped countryside where there was no running water, no electricity, and no supermarkets-where people lived off the land, lived in grass huts, slept on the floor, and grew their own food. Even today, there are people living in parts of Ethiopia just as people lived 2000 years ago! Amazing.

In Ethiopia, we learned a lesson on generosity. We were in Ethiopia for ten days. We had a guide who spoke the native language and took care of us. We were not on a mission trip. We were basically visiting ancient churches and studying the customs and history of Ethiopia. I could write a book just about that trip! We knew most of the people in Ethiopia we would encounter would be poor. We had not visited a third-world country before, so we did not really know what to expect. When we landed at the airport in Addis Ababa, I exchanged some money so that we would have some Ethiopian money to spend and some to give away. I decided to exchange thirty USD into Ethiopian money, the Birr. Currently, there are about 36 Birr for every USD. That means for thirty dollars American money, I received about thirty-six hundred Birr. To put this in perspective, a person can eat for a day on two Birr. That is about three cents in the United States of America! We would give people everywhere we went five to ten Birr. We did this until all the Birr were gone. We gave people what amounted from fifteen to thirty cents. We gave them enough to eat for a few days. How generous we were! Not! When we left the country, my wife and I said to one another, "We could have, should have, done more to be generous." We determined that if we ever had another opportunity like that, we would be more generous.

About ten years ago, we went on a mission trip to Haiti to build an orphanage with the Fuller Center for Housing. The founder of the Fuller Center, Millard Fuller, was the same man who started Habitat for Humanity. We planned on this trip to be much more generous. We collected tools and items of clothing from church members to give away in Haiti. We took an extra suitcase full of items to be given away, and then to give the suitcase away! I decided to give away my work boots and my back brace to one of the workers. I will never forget the look on his face when I tried to convince him that my boots and back brace were his, for free. Since we did not speak their language, I had to enlist one of our guides to explain what I wanted to do. The Haitian workers at that orphanage were paid twenty dollars a week. Not much pay for hard labor in the heat of the day. My gift to that Haitian man amounted to about a month's wages. I wish I would have done more.

My wife and I decided to take as much cash with us as we could. We decided that before we left Haiti, we would give all that money away. After all, once we got on the airplane to fly home, we did not need cash because we had credit cards. One of the men to whom we gave money was one of our guides. He had taken us to the tent city just out of Port-au-Prince, where forty thousand people live. Many of these people had lost their homes in the earthquake that ravaged Haiti some years before our trip. Our guide told us that he had relatives who lived in this tent city. Can you imagine living in tents, with forty thousand people, where there was very little water, no sanitary conditions, and no food? When I gave him the money on our last day of our trip, he stood there staring at the money. He looked at me. He said, "Gift?" I said, "Yes, gift." He began to weep. That money could make a real difference for his family members, maybe even enabling them to move out of the tent city. I wish we would have done more.

At our church, we have had what we called a Free-For-All. That does not mean we had a brawl! It meant we had a rummage sale at the church, and everything was free. We did not want professional rummage people to come to the Free-For-All, pick out the best items and go and sell them for a profit. We wanted to help people who could really benefit from receiving items for free. So, we went to a local food bank and handed out fliers about the Free-For-All. We knew these food banks had screened people and that these people were truly in need. Members of the church donated the items for the Free-For-All. We tried to limit each person who came to the Free-For-All to five items so that no one would try to hoard what was given away. There were furniture items, children's toys, clothes, household goods, and the like. It was wonderful to see that great big room full of free items. We also gave away free food, donuts, and coffee. We had members who walked around the room to help the people who came. One man asked me, as he held up an item, "How much does this cost?" I said, "Nothing." He said, "Nothing?" I said it was absolutely free. If you want it, take it. He said, "Really?" I said, "Really!"

Now we did not receive any new members from those who came to the Free-For-All. That was not the goal. The goal was to be generous to those in need.

At Thanksgiving time, we would contact a local elementary school and tell them we wanted to donate turkeys and a box of groceries to people who were in need. We asked that the school contact the people in advance to get their permission for us to deliver the food to them. The school gave us a list of names and addresses of people who had agreed to receive the food. We would deliver up to eighty turkeys and boxes of food. Funds for the food would be donated by members of the church. Young people would be involved in packing the food boxes. Families would deliver the food on the Sunday afternoon before Thanksgiving.

Again, we did not receive any new members from those who received the food. That was not the goal. The goal was to be generous to those in need.

About twenty years ago, one of our Elders came up with the idea to start a Pastor's Discretionary Fund. On each third Sunday of the month, a special offering would be taken for this fund. Some guidelines were established for the fund. Only the pastor could make decisions about spending money in the fund. The funds could only be used to help people in financial need. The only other people who knew about what was given were the treasurer of the church and one of the Elders, who received monthly reports about the funds. Every penny that was given out, usually by check, was substantiated by a paper trail. If cash was given out, which happened infrequently, the recipient had to sign a voucher for the cash. The funds could be given to members and non-members. The pastor could not receive any of the money, no matter how bad he needed it!

Checks would be written to utility providers, landlords, medical providers, but usually not to individuals. We decided to only help someone one time a year. Over the years, thousands of dollars have been given to this fund. Many people have been helped. Other local churches referred people to our church! The County's Social Services program referred people to our church! Being generous is fun!

I could share many stories about how people have been helped through the Discretionary Fund. I will only share one. This story illustrates how people can be generous to someone in need and be involved in being generous to others through the church. A member of our church became aware of a young lady who lived in a city close to our church. The woman had severe problems with her teeth. She had no dental insurance. She had no money to have her mouth problems fixed. I asked to meet with the woman. Someone had to pick her up and drive her to my office. She came into my office holding a towel in front of her face. She was extremely embarrassed by her appearance. Her health was being compromised because of the poor condition of her teeth. Her self-esteem was low. We decided to help her in the best way possible. After much research, we determined that the best way to help her was to find a dentist that would do the work at a reduced cost. She needed extensive work on her mouth and then to be fitted for dentures. We found a dentist that would do all the work for a total cost of $900. God bless that dentist for his generosity!

After the work had been completed and she had her new dentures, she came to visit me. When she came into my office, she had a great big smile! She said, "Thank you!" I said, "No, thank God because He is the one who made this possible." She did come to worship a couple of times, but the distance for her to come to church made it difficult. Again, we did not help her so that she would become a member of the church. That was not the goal. The goal was to be generous to someone in need.

Generosity is contagious. Generosity goes much further when you partner with other people. We have been blessed to be a blessing. Some ideas to help you on the road of being a new creation in Christ in generosity:

1. Start something at your church where you can help people in need. Will it cost? You bet. Will it be easy? Not hardly. Will it be worth it? Absolutely. One church has a car ministry. People can bring cars in every Saturday to be fixed. Some people have started a ministry to help widows with fix-it jobs in their houses. Find a need and meet it. That takes generosity.

2. Tithe a windfall. If you receive some unexpected income, decide in advance that if this ever happens, you will give a portion of it to help others.

3. Set aside money each month to give away to someone in need. Keep record of what you set aside. It may be fifty or a hundred dollars a month. If you do this, you already know that you have the money to help someone. Just find someone to give it to!

4. When you go to a restaurant, pray about the tip you will give. The server is not spending his/her time and energy to serve you just because they have nothing else to do! My daughter used to work as a server in the restaurant. She said that all the servers hated to work on Sunday

afternoon because that is when the church people come to eat and give lousy tips. The tip one family left her was a witnessing tract. That was their tip. Really? What were you thinking? One family wrote on the restaurant bill that they gave God ten percent of their income, so why would they give a server more than they give God? When at a restaurant, I often ask my wife, "What kind of tip are we going to give?" One time we had a waiter that we learned was from Haiti. The restaurant was pretty empty that day. I told my wife I wanted to give the waiter 100 dollars. The bill for the meal was about $35. She told me that if that is what I felt I should do, go ahead and do it. I did. Before we could reach the door to leave, he ran out to stop us and to thank us for blessing him. I said, "A generous God moved us to be generous to you!" Am I good at being generous? Hardly. I am a work in progress.

Questions to evaluate your generosity:

1. How are you doing at being a new creation in generosity?
2. Who have you helped recently?
3. What are you planning to do to be generous?

We want to be generous because God has been generous to us. God is honored when we are generous. Find someone to help.

CHAPTER TEN

Becoming a New Creation in Our Mortality

A woman who was a member of my church had not been feeling well for some time. She went to her doctor. The doctor admitted her to a local hospital for further tests. Even though this was years ago, I can still see her sitting in her hospital room. Her husband told me the prognosis. His wife had terminal cancer, and there was nothing, medically speaking, that could be done. His wife said, "Pastor, I have always believed that you play the cards you are dealt. That is what I intend to do." She was released from the hospital and died a few days later. She faced her mortality and made peace with it. How about you? Have you dealt with the fact of your mortality?

God is the one who gives us life. He wants us to live life to the full. Notice, He does not promise a full life in the sense of longevity but in quality. We are mortal beings because of sin. There is a time to be born and a time to die. Everyone will one day die. Dealing with that reality in a courageous way, moment by moment, can help us become new creations in Christ.

I have often told people, "You don't know how to live until you know how to die." What do I mean by that? Simply this, you cannot live a full life until you deal with the fact of your mortality. In my ministry, I dealt with a lot of grieving people and a lot of funerals. I even know a lot of the funeral directors by name! I have witnessed many people dealing with death, either their own death or the death of a loved one. I have wept with people who are facing death. I have been in the hospital when people are removed from life support. I have been with couples when their child was stillborn. I have been with couples when their child was born prematurely and had a few minutes to live. I have seen children die in their mother's arms. I have counseled people who are terminal. I have been with families who are gathered around a bedside waiting for a loved one to die. I am well acquainted with death. I never wanted my familiarity with death to cause me to be numb or uncaring about the grief of others. I have sometimes cried with families. I have sometimes been strong with a family when a loved one is dying but wept for them when I left. I have cried when preaching at funerals. Facing death is difficult. You can only face death courageously when you have faith that there is life beyond the grave through faith in Jesus Christ.

My children have heard me talk about death. They know the answer to the following question because they have heard me ask it numerous times. When we would pass a cemetery, I would ask them, "Do you know how many dead people there are in that cemetery?" At first, they would try to guess the number of people that were buried at that cemetery. They know the answer now. How many dead people are there in that cemetery? All of them. And I would say to them, "Of corpse they are." I did not want to make light of death or deny its existence. I wanted my children to face the reality of death and to be prepared to face death with the confidence that comes from the Christian faith. Death is a part of our life. Some of the funerals that I spoke at were for very young people. Some of the funerals I spoke at were for people in old age. Some of the deaths I witnessed were totally unexpected. Some were expected. You never know when your time to die will come. How do you deal with that reality?

First, since none of us knows how long we will live, make the most of each day you have. That does not mean we take the Epicurean philosophy approach-eat, drink, and be merry, for tomorrow we die. That is a philosophy of pleasure. It encourages people to live for the pleasure of each day, no matter the consequences. It also does not mean that we become Stoics. The Stoics teach that you deny all feelings so that nothing will bother you, not even death. That kind of thinking is a recipe for denial. How do you live each day to the fullest? You focus your life on becoming a new creation in Christ. You put into practice the teachings of this book. Better yet, you put into practice the teachings of the Bible.

Next, be ready to die at any age. The fact of the matter is that we are not guaranteed a life of a hundred years. We are mortal. We could die from a disease like Coronavirus. We could die from some accident. We could die because some function in our body falls apart or is attacked by cancer. Years ago, I did a funeral for a twenty-three-year-old man that died from cancer. This young man did not party. He did not smoke or drink. He came from a supportive family. Yet, he got cancer. He fought it to the end. Why does a young man die from cancer? I do not know, except to say that we are all mortal and can die at any time. Be prepared at any age to face the reality of death. There are two things people don't want to talk about, death and taxes. Both are a reality. To ignore the reality of death is foolish. To be ready for death is wise. Prepare your loved ones for the reality that your time on earth has a limit, and you do not know what that limit is. Talk about death. Make peace with it. Don't think that death is only something for older people to deal with.

You can also be ready to die by taking care of the business in your life. Sure, there are legal documents that can help you prepare, a will, power of attorney, advance directives. It is important to take care of the business of the legal matters. It is also important to take care of our relationship with God and our relationships with our loved ones. When facing the reality of our mortality, it is important to deal with any sin in our lives. If we have messed up in some way, ask and receive God's forgiveness. Then seek to make a change. Take care of damaged relationships. Don't wait until your deathbed to talk to people from whom you are estranged. Reach out to them. Do all that you can do to make amends. Death may come quickly, and you may not have time to take care of this kind of business. Do it now.

Lastly, settle the question about where you will spend eternity. Everyone will live forever. We were created with a soul. Our soul is eternal. The Bible says that when we die, we are absent from the body and present with the Lord (2 Corinthians 5:6-8). When we die, we can be present with the Lord if we are a believer in Christ as our Savior from sin and death. All people will die, and all people will live beyond the grave. The only question is, where will you be? Jesus promised that all who believe in Him as their Savior will pass from this life to eternal life in heaven. There is no other way to go to heaven than by faith in Jesus Christ. You can make peace with death if you know that death is not the end; it is a new beginning. You will go to heaven, not because you have been a good person, but because Jesus paid for the forgiveness of your sin and for you to go to heaven. Jesus said in John 14:6, "No one comes to the Father (to heaven) but by me." Pretty straightforward.

Being a new creation in Christ means that you are never, at any time in your life, afraid of death. It means you can stare death in the face and say, "Where O Death is your victory?" (1 Corinthians 15:55)

Questions to evaluate how you are coping with your mortality:

1. Can you talk to loved ones about death?
2. Are you sure where you will spend eternity?
3. Are you fearful of death?
4. Are you living each day to the fullest?

Grow in becoming a new creation in Christ in your mortality.

CHAPTER ELEVEN

Becoming a New Creation Morally

Recently, I went to a store to purchase several items. When I finished paying the bill, I took the items to my car and loaded them in the back seat. When I got in my car, I glanced at the receipt. The cashier had not charged me for three items. What should I do?

In college, I gave a girl a ride back to her dormitory after a school function. I was studying to be a pastor, and her father was a pastor. It was dark. It was cold outside. When I parked at the dormitory, she took my hand and said she liked me. She was very pretty. Then she leaned over to me as if she wanted a kiss. At that time, I was engaged to be married to another girl back in Florida. What should I do?

In high school, some students put together an end-of-the-year party at a lake West of town. I had asked a girl to go on a date with me. She agreed. We went and got something to eat. Then I told her about this party West of town and asked her if she wanted to go. She said it was fine with her. When I drove to the lake, there was a group of maybe one hundred students already there. It was obvious some of the students there had been drinking. One young man had a great deal to drink. All of a sudden, he yelled out, "Let's go skinny dipping!" With that, he proceeded to take his clothes off. What should I do?

Several years ago, I visited a woman at her house to talk with her about a matter regarding one of her children. Her husband was at work. The children were at school. She subtly suggested that we were adults and could have an affair. No one needed to know. What should I do?

Life is made up of many choices. We can choose to live by the flesh (our sinful nature) or the Spirit. God wants to help us make right choices. At the end of the day, did we choose to do something different than what we normally would do because God showed us what is good and right? These choices, based upon the standards and values of God, will help us become new creations morally.

I do not want this chapter to be a list of legalistic things of what is wrong and what is right. The Bible is not clear about what we should do in every situation. We have to resist the urge to want a rule book for living. We have to resist the urge to prescribe to other people how they should live. But if we love God, we will want to please Him in our choices. We will want to honor Him in what we do. We will want to be new creations in Christ. This is not easy. It is difficult to discern the will of God in every situation. There are so many choices. Some choices are clear. Some choices are black and white. For instance, it is wrong to have an affair when you are married. It is wrong to desire to hurt or kill someone. It is wrong to lie to someone so that you can profit. But some choices are not black or white. They are gray. If a salesman is trying to sell a car, should he try to get the best profit margin he can get, or should he sell the car at the best bargain the buyer can get? What kind of clothes should someone wear to church? What kind of worship format should be used in a church? Is it okay to pray without folding your hands? What kind of food can a person eat? Can we have friends that are not Christians? Gray areas. The Bible does not speak to every issue. It takes discernment to choose what is right.

I would like to give some general principles to help you navigate the gray areas of life. They are not all-encompassing. Finally, if we are to choose what is the right thing to do in the gray areas of life, we must develop a sensitivity to the Holy Spirit. The Holy Spirit lives in us if we are believers in Christ. The Spirit knows the mind of God. The Spirit can help us make right choices. Often this happens when the Spirit nudges us in our stomach. When you don't feel right about something, listen to the Spirit. When you know the right thing to do, even if it is difficult, do the right thing. That is what it means to be a new creation in Christ.

If we want to obey the Spirit of God, we resist the urge to cut corners. There are almost always ways to cut corners. Sometimes we can be more efficient by working smarter rather than harder. That is not what I am talking about. When we cheapen the quality of our work, when we do not do the job correctly in order to save some money or make the job go quicker, we are cutting corners and not doing what is right. We are not being new creations in Christ. The janitor that sweeps some dirt under a rug, is cutting corners. The roofer that does not put the required number of nails in each shingle is cutting corners. The painter that thins the paint so that he can make more money by using less material is cutting corners. The pastor that does not spend time in study of the Word of God and prayer when he is preparing his message for God's people is cutting corners. People may not know that you did a substandard job. It may be hidden for a while. But God knows. And we know. Don't settle for what is not right.

A few months ago, I worked with my son, Stephen, on a fence. He has a side business building fences. The fence we were constructing was about 150 feet long. The fence looked good. Really good. Then we were to build a gate that would link the fence to the house. It was a double gate that went up a hill to the house. When the gate was done, you could not open the gate all the way. The hill blocked the fence from opening all the way. The hill was covered with stones to keep the dirt from eroding away from the house. My son decided to remove the stones and dig out the hill so the gate would open. It took more time to remove the stones. It took more time to dig out the hill. He had to go to a store and purchase more stones. But he said, "I want it to look like it was designed that way from the beginning." He could lay his head down at night and know that he did the best that he could with that fence. He did not cut corners. That is worth something. It is worth something to God.

If we want to make the right decisions, it is vital to establish the criteria for what is right and what is wrong. We all have to do this. We have to draw a line between what is right and what is wrong. Once we do this, we know what to do. We will stay on the right side of the line. In our culture today, the lines are blurred or not existent at all. People do whatever they want to do or feel like doing in the moment. There is no line. Anything goes. That is not how God wants His people to live.

I know a bank vice-president that lost his job because he would not do something that his boss wanted him to do because it was unethical. Maybe what he was being required to do was not illegal, but it was unethical. He drew a line. When an actress does not take part in a movie because the script would require her to do something against her morals, she is drawing a line. When a young person decides not to live with a partner before marriage or to save sex before marriage, he/she is drawing a line. When older people do not live together outside of marriage just because it is financially more advantageous, they are drawing a line. When a church worker decides not to go out to lunch alone with a person of the opposite sex, he/she is drawing a line. When a shopper receives too much change back from the cashier and talks to the cashier about the error, making it right, he/she is drawing a line. Where are your lines? It is a scary thing to drive down a road in the dark during a blinding rainstorm where you cannot see the lines. It is also perilous to go through life without any lines between what is bad and good. God will help us draw the lines. God will help us stay on the right side. The more we let God do that, the more we become new creations in Christ.

A helpful guideline I have used with people in counseling is to drive a particular thought or decision to its logical extreme. In other words, if everyone thought the way we did, or behaved the way we did, what would be the result? This is one way to check our thinking. Does the logical extreme of what we are thinking lead to a place we want to be? Does it lead to a decision that God would be pleased with? If everyone decided to loot businesses and riot when things didn't go their way, what would happen? If everyone was unfaithful to their spouse, what would happen? If everyone gave up when the going got tough, what would happen? You can see what I mean. Extrapolate the thought to its logical conclusion and see what can happen. This is a way to check our thoughts and choices and reign them in. It is a way to develop good morals or a way to make decisions about how we want to live.

We can go far along the road of good morals if we make our word our bond. Scammers and schemers have forked tongues. You cannot really believe what they say. Unfortunately, many of us know people who work in the service trades, plumbers, carpenters, air conditioning technicians, and the like, tell a customer they will be there to do a job on a Monday. Monday comes and goes, and the worker is a no-show. They do not call the customer either. They can have all kinds of excuses for not keeping their word. But it reveals their true character. If you make a commitment to do something at a particular time and find out that you are not going to be able to do what you said, call the person and explain to them why you are not able to keep your word.

If you are selling a used car to someone, tell them everything that is wrong with that car. The buyer will find out anyway, that is, if they buy the car. Sure, it may mean you may lose the sale. It may cost you something. But you will be honest. Telling the truth can be costly. Tell the truth anyway.

No one makes right choices all the time. I have made a bunch of bad decisions. When you do make a bad decision, own it. Admit it. Confess it and seek to make it right. Above all, learn from it. That process is what life in Christ is all about. As we become new creations in Christ, we draw lines, we establish what is right and wrong, we keep our word, and we learn and grow from our mistakes.

If I were to ask you to make a list of ten moral principles that govern your life, would you be able to list ten? Try it. List ten lines between good and bad that you have drawn in your life. What would they be? Write them out. See if you can list ten things that guide your life in becoming a new creation in Christ.

Ask yourself:

1. Do I have a moral standard by which I live?
2. Do I cut corners when doing a job?
3. Do I keep my word?
4. Do I seek wisdom from the Holy Spirit to cultivate good morals?

CHAPTER TWELVE

Becoming a New Creation in Your Self-Esteem

There is a great deal being written today about having good self-esteem. However, it is better to have good God-esteem. We become a new creation in Christ when we see ourselves as God sees us. When you look in the mirror, what do you see? Do you see yourself by the standard of the world? Do you compare yourself to others? We all compare ourselves to others to some degree. But if we define who we are by our comparison to others, we will shortchange our value and worth. Listen, a pimple does not define who you are. Your bottom line, financially speaking, does not determine who you are. Your parents' dysfunction does not define who you are. What others think about you does not define who you are. God defines who you are. God made you special, unique. God redeemed you by the death of His Son, Jesus Christ. God-esteem means you see yourself as God sees you, and you do not let anyone or anything come against that.

Again, when you look in the mirror, what do you see? What we see seems to be reality. It has been said, seeing is believing.

So, if you see yourself as being inadequate, as damaged goods, as defective in some way, you will think that your perception is really how you are. Your perception about yourself, real or not, can become a self-fulfilling prophecy. You will, usually without even realizing it, live your life in such a way that you project your perceived reality into your life. You will expect things to be a certain way, so you will live in such a way that what you see about yourself will be proved by the outcome of your life. God wants to totally change your perception of yourself so that you do not settle for less of what you can become. God wants you to be a new creation in Christ.

If a young girl has a perceived rejection from her father, she may begin to live her life as a response to that rejection. If her father does not compliment her on her looks, she may begin to see herself as not being very pretty. If her father does not have time for her, she may begin to feel that she is not very important. If her father is critical when he is with her, if he does not give acceptance and approval but instead puts her down, she instinctively incorporates some coping mechanisms into her thinking to help her deal with the hurt and rejection she feels. She may allow some guy to treat her poorly because she believes that is all she deserves. She has believed a lie about herself. How much better to see yourself as God sees you and to live with God's perspective of who you are, since our perception of self, as defined by others, can sometimes fall short of how God sees us.

The tendency, in my experience, is that a girl who feels unloved and rejected by her father will do one of three dysfunctional things to cope with her pain. She could act out in a rebellious way to show by her rebellion that she does not care about what her father or anyone thinks about her. Her rebellion can also be a way to punish her father for his perceived rejection. Acting out the pain can be manifested in promiscuity, self-cutting, addictions, or dysfunctional relationships. Her pain is therefore manifested in her manner of life.

Another way to cope with the pain of feeling rejected and unloved is to simply numb out, to not feel anything. Life then consists of just going through the motions. If she does not feel anything, she cannot hurt or be hurt. In this numb state, she does not really enjoy doing anything. She does not get upset when she is wronged. She has no goals or visions for her life. It is a "safe" way to live, but it is not really living at all.

The third way to cope with the pain of rejection is to internalize the pain. When emotional pain is internalized, it will seek a way to manifest itself in a person's life. Pain will stick out somewhere in the person's life. The pain within may lead the person to feel that they need to be punished because something must be wrong with them to be treated so poorly. They may become obsessive in some area of life, trying to measure up to the expectations of the person causing the pain. Some people evidence eating disorders. They think, "If I am not pretty, then I need to lose weight, no matter what." They may go to the other extreme and feel that food makes them feel loved, so why not eat? Some people turn to achievement, whether in academic studies or at work. Workaholics work until they are exhausted and don't have to deal with their pain. Alcohol, drug, or porn addictions are a way people deal with their pain. Some people give in to some sort of religious obsession. Their religious practices consume their life. This is the most subtle one of all. After all, how can you criticize someone who is always at church, always praying, always trying to do the things that please God? What really drives them is a desire to overcome their pain. Obviously, it is not a healthy way to live.

What a person "sees" about themselves can be a very powerful influence in a person's life. Often the person does not realize why they do the things that they do. They feel frustrated, ashamed, and confused, but they do not understand why they feel this way. What someone grew up with seems normal to them because that is all they have known. Abused children often allow themselves to be abused when they grow up. Neglected children often keep people at a distance when they become adults. Children who grew up in angry families often become angry adults. God wants to change how we see ourselves and how we see other people. God wants us to see ourselves as loved and capable of loving others. God can help us see ourselves as new creations in Christ. As the Bible says, "The old has been done away with, the new has come" (2 Corinthians 5:17).

What are some of the results of a negative view of ourselves? What are the symptoms of a false perception of reality? We will look at some of these and then look at what a healthy self-perception looks life. What does it look like to think of ourselves as new creations in Christ? I hope you are able to do some honest evaluation about what is really going on in your life. It takes work. It can be very painful. But sometimes, the working through of the underlying issues behind why we do what we do can produce great healing and growth. Do the work. It is part of becoming a new creation in Christ.

Negative self-esteem factors:

1. When we let failure define who we are. Have I failed? You bet. I have not always been the husband to my wife that I could have been. I did not always parent my children in a way that pleased the Lord. Sometimes I got angry with my children. One night I went into my son's room to pray with him before he went to bed. My son was about ten at the time. I could tell that he had not brushed his teeth before coming to bed. So, I told him to go and brush his teeth. He reluctantly got up, marched into the bathroom, ran his toothbrush across his teeth, and threw his toothbrush at the bathroom mirror. He was not happy that I made him get out of bed and brush his teeth. I was not happy that he had splattered the mirror with toothpaste. So, I picked him up by his arms, holding him at eye level against the wall. He started to cry. I asked him why he was crying since I was not holding him too tightly in order to hurt him. He said, "There is a nail in my back." When I moved him, sure enough, there was a nail in the wall where a picture once hung, and it was in his back. I had to apologize to him for my behavior. Have I failed? You bet. And so have you. But our failures do not define who we are. Failure is not final. Because Jesus died for us, there is plenty of forgiveness for all our failures. Put your failures in the past and move on. Learn from your failures.

2. We have a wrong perception of reality when we compare ourselves to others. We are not like others. That is not a value statement. It is a statement of fact. God has made each of us unique. We are not like others. God wants us to be the best that we can be, not to try to be like other people. I had to relearn this lesson a couple of years ago when I was playing golf with some guys that were much younger than me. I wanted to drive the ball as far as they drove the ball. When that was my goal, my golf game became pretty ugly. I could not hit the ball like they were hitting the ball. When I decided to just do what I could do, the best that I could do it, even if the ball did not go as far, the game went much better. Avoid the comparison game. It only leads to frustration. Just be the best you can be with what God has given you.

3. *We have a wrong perception of reality when we allow boundary violations in our relationships with others.* A boundary violation is when we cash in who we are in order to appease another person. When we let other people control our thoughts, feelings, or decisions, that is a boundary violation. When we feel coerced, guilted, manipulated, or shamed, we are dealing with a boundary violation. People who have good God-esteem feel secure in who they are. They stick up for themselves. They communicate to others, "My feelings and thoughts are important, and I have every right to talk about them in a calm, loving way." Doing that sets good boundaries. We have to draw good boundaries in our relationships, or we will lose sight of who we are. It may seem right to please another person who tries to control us, but that is a wrong perception of reality. Sometimes the right thing to do is to say no. You can say it in a nice way. But you can say no.

4. *We have a wrong perception of reality when we listen to the echoes of the past and let them determine how we live in the present.* We all do this to some degree. The echoes of the past are things

people have said to us that have hurt us in some way. These echoes reverberate in our minds. These echoes can color how we see things in the present and alter how we deal with things in the present. For instance, I know a father who said to his children when they made a mistake, spilled some milk, dropped something, "You knucklehead." Another father said to his son, "You will never amount to anything." A mother said to her daughter, "There are pretty girls, and you are not one of them. Get used to it." These kinds of comments can really hurt. They can echo in our minds our whole life long. Any echo from the past that causes us to magnify a current event or solicits a disproportionate response to a current event is a signal that we are letting the echo, the hurt wins the day. Identify the hurtful things that people have said to you in the past and determine to not let them define who you are or how you live.

5. *We have a wrong perception of reality if we focus too much on the negative.* There will always be problems in life. There will always be things that are negative. But these negative things are not the only way to gauge our life. If we focus too much on the negative, we will not be able to see the positive. There are always good things going on in our life as well.

6. *We have a wrong perception of reality if we think a setback today affects our whole life.* Loss does not mean you are a loser. If someone loses his/her job, it does not mean his/her life is finished. It may feel that way in the present, but that is not the truth. There are other jobs. The loss of a job does not define your life. Many times, the loss of a job leads to something even better! The loss of a marriage does not define your life. One

Sunday morning, I was in my office at the church, and I got a knock on my door. When I opened the door, I saw a man I knew, disheveled and distraught. When he came home from work on Friday, the police were in his driveway. He asked them what was going on. They arrested him for domestic violence. On Saturday, he had gotten out of jail and, during the night, slept in his car in the church parking lot, not knowing what to do. He could not go home due to a restraining order. His words were, "What gave my life meaning is now all gone." That is how he felt at that moment. But that was not the end of the story. He moved on. He got his life back together. He did not let that unfortunate setback define his life. In every loss, there are powerful lessons that can be learned in no other way. God has a plan for your life. Don't get stuck in the heartache of the moment. Believe that God will take care of you and lead you out of your present situation to something new and different. Trust Him to take you to that new thing.

Enough about life events that can affect our self-esteem in a negative way. There are some positive ways of thinking that, if we see them, will give our life meaning and empower us to handle just about anything. I have chosen to frame these positive ways of thinking in terms related to retail stores. I hope the analogy will be helpful when thinking about what you have going for you as you put your trust in God.

Positive God-esteem factors:

1. Take inventory of your support system. Businesses take regular inventory of their stock. This is how they reorder their inventory or decide what inventory is not moving and needs to be changed. You can do the same in your relationships. There are people who genuinely care about you. They will stand beside you. You are not alone. You have a support system. Draw strength from that fact, even when you may feel that you are alone.

Several years ago, a woman called me and told me goodbye. I asked if she was going on a trip, and if so, where to? She did not give me a clear answer. So, I told her I was coming over to her house so that we could talk. I immediately went over to her house. She opened up to me and began to share what was going on in her life. She said she was planning to commit suicide and that she had it all planned out. Her plan involved a bowl of ice and a razor blade. She said her life seemed like a drop in the ocean. She felt that if she no longer lived, no one would notice or care. What she believed at that moment was not true. I asked her to do an inventory of people who genuinely cared about her. I told her there were a great many people that cared about her. The people at her job cared. Her parents were still alive at that time, and I knew they cared. I told her people at the church cared about her. I told her I cared about her. But most important of all, God cared about her!

After we did an inventory of people that cared about her, I asked her to promise me that she would not do anything to harm herself that night. She promised me she would not harm herself that day. I asked her to give me all of her razor blades, which she did. I called her the next day and asked her to again promise that she would not harm herself, which she did.

Although she never married, she eventually adopted a little girl from a country in South America. She raised the girl and lived a long life. She took inventory of her support system, and it changed her life.

2. *Affix proper value to yourself.* Sometimes people feel that they are not worth much. Who switched the price tags? Our worth is not determined by our position, possessions, or popularity. God has established our worth. God gave His highest possession, His only begotten Son, for you. The blood of Christ shed for you on the cross is beyond any earthly value. God thinks you are worth a great deal!

Any item is worth whatever value people place on it. Recently my wife and I went to an antique store in North Carolina. The store was actually a two-story house that was filled with antiques. There was a picture of Elvis, a photograph, for sale for fifty dollars. Let me give you some advice. There are thousands of pictures of Elvis on the internet, many of them available for free. That picture of Elvis was only worth fifty dollars if someone would pay fifty dollars for it! There were old milk bottles, you know, the kind the milkman used to deliver milk to your door every morning. I am dating myself now! Those old milk bottles were worth only the amount that someone would pay for them. There were old farm tools. Who would want old rusty farm tools? How much are they really worth? The point is, things are worth what someone will pay for them. God paid the supreme price for you. Therefore, you are worth a great deal. Why? Because God says so. What God says is infinitely more important than what some magazine or some pundit may say about you.

3. *Determine the quality of how you were made.* Things that are made well cost more. Things that are made poorly tend to be cheap. When God made you, He made a quality product. You are fearfully and wonderfully made (Psalm 139:14). God formed you in the womb of your mother. God was directly involved in your creation. God would not make you of inferior quality. God has designed the cells of your body to carry out specific functions. You are fearfully and wonderfully made. God created your organs to keep you going, and they work wonderfully. God gave you a brain and a nervous system so that you could create things and express yourself. God gave you a soul, that eternal dimension of your existence where you can relate to God. God made you uniquely male or female. Think about that! God did not say at your birth, oops, messed up on that one. No way! Each person is a different creation of God. Each person displays God's handiwork. You are not perfect because of the fall into sin. But you are nonetheless a special creation of God.

God made you unique. You don't have the gifts and skills of everyone else. But God has given you certain skills to do some things. Realistically, I may not be able to do all the things other people can do. But I can accomplish many home projects. I am a fix-it person. Some things I fix pretty well. Others I don't fix as well. I am not a professional carpenter. I am not a professional floor tile layer. I am not a professional drywall finisher. I am a professional roofer, though! I am not a professional at everything, but that is okay. I have the satisfaction of doing handiwork myself and saving a great deal of money. Since God made you with unique skills, do the best with what you have. Use your God-given abilities to do what you can do. God is pleased with that!

4. Another positive self-esteem quality is to show up, step up and speak up. You may not feel like going to work on a particular day, but you show up because you made a commitment to show up. In other words, don't get stuck in your feelings. Your feelings are not the boss of you. If you are working for an employer, your feelings are not your boss, your boss is! And if you are the boss in your job, then God is your boss! And God says that you are to show up! I have a health club membership. Sometimes I do not feel like working out. But I know that if I just show up, I will get the workout. Just get yourself there.

When there is a task that no one else will do, step up. You may not have all the answers as to how the task needs to be done, but if you step up, God will show you the way. I have often asked people to serve in the church in some way. I heard repeatedly from people that they did not know how to do what I was asking them to do. They said, "I have never done that before." My response was, "Everyone has to start somewhere. We will teach you how to do it. Just step out of the boat and trust that God will walk you through it." Step up. Step out in faith and let God lead you. Don't get stuck where you are. Step up and try the new thing. Stepping out in faith will move you out of your comfort zone. Stepping out in faith will put you in a position where you have to trust God. When you step out and you are doing something God wants you to do, God will supply what you need to handle the new venture.

Sometimes you need to speak up. When you speak up, you are making a commitment. You are defining yourself. You are acting on faith. Speak up. You might not be listened to when you speak up. Speak up anyway. Joshua spoke up to the people of God. He said in Joshua 24:15, "But if serving the LORD seems undesirable to you, then choose for yourselves this day whom you will serve, whether the gods your ancestors served beyond the Euphrates or the gods of the Amorites, in whose land you are living. But as for me and my household, we will serve the LORD." Joshua spoke up, and the people responded to his message.

While in college, I came home for two and a half months one summer. I needed a job so that I could make some money. I could not find a job. It seemed the other college students had come home before I arrived and already had taken the available jobs. I saw the office of a roofing company. I had never worked in roofing. I said to myself, why not go into the office and apply for a job? I started that job the next day. That roofing company paid the workers an hourly wage. I was twenty-one years of age at the time. After two weeks of working for that company, I asked to speak to the owner of the company. I went into his office, sat in front of his desk, and asked for a raise. He looked at me over his glasses, glared at me would be a better way to say it. I told him I was a hard worker, that I was just as fast at laying shingles as the other workers, and that he could ask the foreman if that was true or not. He yelled, "Get out of my office!" Which I did. The next Friday, I got a raise. If I had not spoken up, I doubt I would have been given that job. If I had not spoken up, I doubt I would have been given that raise. Speak up. Believe in yourself.

5. *All retail stores, if they are selling anything, have to restock the shelves.* When you have depleted the resources of your energy, restock your shelves. When you have done everything that you know to do and don't know what to do next, restock the shelves. When a door is closed, and you feel an emptiness in your life, place a new order. You restock the shelves when you continue to hear the Word of God and build up your faith. The shelf of goods in your life is your faith. If you have empty shelves, you have little faith. If your shelves are full, you have great faith. Restock the shelves often. Go to a church. Practice regular devotions. Listen to teachings on the internet. Talk to God in prayer and listen to what God has to say. Restock the shelves. When your shelves are stocked, you will have a great deal to offer to other people.

6. *Another positive self-esteem quality is the ability to change the station.* Have you noticed when you go into a store that there is music playing? Music has a profound influence on our lives. So does what you listen to on a daily basis. What you listen to becomes a dominant factor in your thinking. I have heard people recently say that they limit how much news they listen to. The news is basically negative and defeating. It is not wrong to listen to the news. What is unhealthy is to listen to the news excessively. Most of the time, the news reports people at their worst. People committing crimes, people doing horrendous

things to others and their property. The political news is very caustic. One party attacks another party. One politician maligns another politician. If that is what you are constantly feeding your mind, your mind will get overloaded only with the negative aspects of society.

My wife listens to podcasts of several Christian ministries while she works on various projects at home. She listens to Christian music while she works. She sometimes says to me, "Turn the news off. It just gets me down." She is changing the station and choosing to listen to what is uplifting and positive.

If you go into a store, you will hear music. You will also hear music at the dentist's office. Go figure! The idea in the store is that when you listen to a certain kind of music, you will feel more motivated to feel good and therefore to make a purchase. When you go to the dentist, the music is intended to relax you and take your mind off the cleaning, scraping, and drilling. When you are neither at a store or the dentist, you have a choice about what station you will listen to! When you change the station to something more positive, you are, in effect, saying: this is who I want to be and what I want to focus on. To think that sometimes a simple choice, like changing the station to something more uplifting, can radically change your life. Change the station. Choose to be a new creation in Christ. When the negativity of the world resounds all around you, change the station to what builds you up in the Lord.

Application questions:

1. Do you let past failures define who you are today?
2. Do you often compare yourself to others?
3. Do you have boundary violations in your relationships with others?
4. Do you let hurtful echoes from the past affect your life today?
5. Are you too negative about your life and others?
6. Do you let setbacks determine your attitude about your future?
7. Do you have a strong support system in your life?
8. Do you think you have intrinsic worth that no one can take from you?
9. Do you chose to focus on your unique gifts, that you are fearfully and wonderfully made?
10. Do you show up, step up, and speak up because you believe in yourself?
11. Do you feed your mind positive truth or allow the negativity of the world to consume your mind?

Conclusion

Becoming a new creation in Christ involves change. If we want to become new creations in Christ throughout our life, it means that we allow God to change our thinking, our habits, our thoughts, emotions, decisions, all of us, so that we become more like Christ. This process of becoming a new creation in Christ is not easy. Many people who name Christ as their Lord will not get involved in the process of becoming a new creation in Christ. Many people will make little changes and think they are becoming a new creation in Christ. Many people will change things in their life outwardly, but not inwardly. If you are not happy with your job and find another job, you are changing things outwardly. If you are not happy in your marriage and get a divorce and a new partner, you are changing things outwardly. If you are not happy with your appearance and buy a new set of clothing, you are changing things outwardly. Real change happens inwardly. Real change takes place when there is a transformation in someone's life. Real change takes place when someone grows in their relationship with God and their understanding of God's truth.

Everyone, young and old people, have role models. We see people that have character traits that we admire, and we want to be like those people. Years ago, young men wanted to be like the great basketball player, Michael Jordan. In fact, there was a television commercial that said, "Be like Mike." Young people want to become Astronauts or the President of the United States. Astronauts and Presidents are their role models. Some young adults want to be like their parents. Their parents are their role models. Some people want to be like some spiritual leader they know, a pastor, teacher, or famous evangelist. We all have people we want to emulate in our lives. Who has been the role models in your life? Who have you known, when you looked at them, you said, "I want to be like that?" Do you have any role models currently in your life? Earlier in this book, I wrote about a pastor I knew when I was a teenager, Rev. Otto Diefenbach. Pastor Diefenbach was loved by the people in his church. He was never critical of others. He treated people with grace. I thought to myself, as a young person, *I want to be like that.* Who are the role models in your life?

Becoming a new creation in Christ means Jesus is your role model. Jesus was the perfect Son of God. The apostle Paul wrote in 2 Corinthians 5:21, "God made him who had no sin to be sin for us so that in Him we might become the righteousness of God." Since Jesus did not sin, He made the right decisions, and He handled people correctly. We can learn a great deal about living correctly from the example of Jesus.

One of the reasons teachers in Jesus' day developed a following of people was so that those people could spend time with the teacher, listen to the teacher, watch the teacher, and become more like the teacher. Jesus chose twelve men to be His disciples. In the Greek language, the word "disciple" means to be a learner. A disciple follows the teacher so that he can learn how to be like that teacher. Today, anyone who is a Christian is a disciple of Jesus. Christians want to learn from the Bible and from the Holy Spirit how to be more like Jesus. Thankfully, the four Gospels in the New Testament tell us a great deal about Jesus. The Gospels were written by men who had studied Jesus. Matthew and John traveled with Jesus as part of the original twelve disciples. Mark wrote his Gospel primarily based on the teaching and testimony of the Apostle Peter, one of the original disciples. Luke wrote his Gospel on the basis of the testimony of many eyewitnesses, people who had been with Jesus (Luke 1:2). Obviously, these books were based on the testimony of people who had been with Jesus, seen the miracles he performed, listened to His teaching, and saw the way He handled many different situations. We have a great resource in becoming more like Christ by studying these four Gospels.

The apostle Paul was confronted by Jesus on the road to Damascus. You can read about that in Acts, chapter 9. Paul admitted that he received the Gospel by revelation from Jesus Christ (Galatians 1:12). God revealed Jesus to Paul (Galatians 1:16). Paul spent fifteen days with Peter, the apostle (Galatians 1:18). Then Paul spent some time with James, the Lord's brother. James became a believer in Jesus as the Son of God after the resurrection (Galatians 1:19). Paul, who wrote much of the New Testament, learned from Jesus. Paul was also guided by the Holy Spirit to be a new creation in Christ. We can learn a great deal from The apostle Paul about being a new creation in Christ.

God, the Father, had it in His mind that those who became believers in Christ would become like Jesus. In Romans 8:28, you find these words about God, "For those God foreknew He also predestined to be conformed to the likeness of His Son, that He might be the first born among many brothers. God wants us to be like His Son, Jesus.

In the Old Testament, to some degree, God was hidden from most people. The Bible describes a veil that hid people from the full revelation of God. In Christ, that veil has been taken away. In 2 Corinthians 3:18, The apostle Paul describes it this way, "And we, who with unveiled faces all reflect the Lord's glory, are being transformed into his likeness with ever-increasing glory, which comes from the Lord, who is the Spirit." So, you see, our role model in life, Jesus, can be clearly seen. The question is whether we will allow the Holy Spirit to transform us into the likeness of Christ. Some people, who are Christians, don't care very much about being like Christ. They are pretty satisfied with the way they are, so why change? Some people want to be like Christ in certain areas of their life, but not in every area. They only want to be like Christ in areas where they feel comfortable. Some people genuinely seek to become like Christ in every area of their life. What about you? How important is it to you to become a new creation in Christ? In what areas of your life would you say God has changed you so that you are becoming more like Christ? I am asking God to help me to be more patient with other people. I want to be more patient with drivers that drive slowly or look like they don't know what to do when they drive. I help an older lady, paying her bills, listening to her, fixing things around her trailer. I realize whenever

I am talking with her or helping her, the task will take ten times longer than it normally would. She has issues. I need an infusion of patience from God when I am dealing with her. I need patience while waiting in the store checkout line. I need patience when waiting in a traffic jam. What character quality of Christ are you working on?

Many years ago, there was a campaign in the Christian church that sought to help people become more like Christ. There were bracelets, necklaces, T-shirts, bumper stickers, and other products that had imprinted on them, WWJD. People were encouraged to ask themselves in each and every situation, What Would Jesus Do? If you are struggling with a relationship, ask, what would Jesus do? If you are feeling downhearted or discouraged in your life, ask, what would Jesus do? If you have to make an important decision in your life, ask, what would Jesus do?

Sometimes the answer to the question, what would Jesus do, can be very difficult. But, if you sort out the answer to that question, by the guidance of the Holy Spirit, and you know the answer, you can be at peace. You will know you are operating in the will of God. When you are in the will of God, you can never be wrong. There is great peace and power when you know you are in the will of God.

The longer I seek to know the will of God in any particular situation, the easier it is to discern the will of God. When you consistently seek to know the will of God, you develop a greater sensitivity to the Holy Spirit. Be sure of this, the will of God may not always make rational sense. Who has completely known the mind of the Lord (Romans 11:34)? The answer? No one. But the Holy Spirit knows the mind of the Lord. The Holy Spirit searches all things, even the deep things of God (1 Corinthians 2:10). The Holy Spirit is working around the clock to direct us into the will of God. The Holy Spirit wants to help us make an inward change. This inward change involves us becoming more like Christ.

As I said earlier, some of the things the Holy Spirit directs us into do not make rational sense. While I was serving as a pastor at a church in Baton Rouge, Louisiana, I was offered a position to be an assistant pastor at a church in Merritt Island, Florida. If I accepted this new position, it would mean I would be serving at a much smaller church without a Christian school. I had children that could attend a Christian school. I would also be going to a church that was not stable financially. I would also be taking a significant reduction in salary. What should I do? My wife and I prayed about this decision one night until early in the morning. We were to give an answer to the church in Merritt Island the next day. We wanted to hear from the Holy Spirit. By the way, decisions in the church should not be driven by money. They should be driven by the Holy Spirit. Some decisions in the church may not make much sense rationally, but if they are from the Holy Spirit, they are the right decisions. Outwardly, it felt this move was not a good decision. Inwardly, my wife and I both felt this change was in the will of God. So, we followed the Spirit's leading. We moved to Merritt Island. God blessed our ministry there. We served at that church for thirty-two years. Here is the point. God knows more than we do. God simply wants us to trust Him and follow the leading of the Holy Spirit.

Will we always get it right when we believe we are following the will of God? Not hardly. But hopefully, we learn from our mistakes and grow in the ability to better discern the will of God. Even in trial and error, the Holy Spirit can lead us. If we are willing to listen and to learn. It is not always an easy process. But it is the best process. It is a vital part of becoming a new creation in Christ.

One of the things we are dealing with in our lives has been a difficult situation. We have a neighbor who is in need of emotional and financial support. We are seeking the will of God as to what we are to do. It is not the will of God to do nothing. Sometimes, it is not the will of God to do everything. To take care of the problems of someone can be simply enabling them to keep being irresponsible. How do you sort out the difference between doing nothing and enabling poor choices? It is not always easy. We can only make the right decision by the guidance of the Holy Spirit.

We have a neighbor who is from Haiti. She is a nice girl but has had a very tough life. Currently, she is a single mother with two children. We have mowed her yard. Her fence had blown down. Although it was the responsibility of the landlord to fix the fence, I fixed the fence. We have taken her son to school and picked him up from school. Her car is broken down. The mechanic who worked on the car said it would take more money to fix the car than the car is worth. What is the will of God in this situation? What does the Spirit of God want us to do or not do? We have prayed about this a lot.

In the next few weeks, this woman will be receiving some money in the form of a stimulus payment. She will also be receiving her Income Tax refund. We decided it was the will of God for us to add to those funds and to help her purchase a car. She really needs a car. We could have said it was not our responsibility to bail her out. Partly, she is in a tough situation because of the bad choices she has made. But God said to us, "Since I have blessed you, why can't you be a blessing to someone in need, even if they don't deserve it?" God has blessed us even though we don't deserve it. In this way, we can be like God. In the Book of Philippians 2, verse 5, Paul says, "Your attitude should be the same as that of Christ Jesus." When your attitude is like Jesus, you are becoming more like Christ.

As part of our morning devotions, my wife and I have been studying the Book of Ephesians. In Ephesians, chapter 4, verses 11-13, you find these words:

> "It was He who gave some to be apostles, some to be prophets, some to be evangelists, and some to be pastors and teachers, to prepare God's people for works of service, so that the body of Christ may be built up until we all reach unity in the faith and in the knowledge of the Son of God and become mature, attaining to the whole measure of the fullness of Christ."

God is working through the church so that we grow in the knowledge of the Son of God and become mature, attaining to the whole measure of the fullness of Christ. What is the whole measure of the fullness of Christ? It means we are in the process of becoming a new creation in Christ. This process means we need to change. We don't bend God to our will. We submit our will to God. We have to change. How have you been changing in the last month or so to become more like Christ? If you cannot think of anything that is being changed, my guess is that you are not changing. In what area of your life do you need peace from God? What person in your life are you seeking to love, even though you do not feel love for that person? What thought patterns are you changing? How are you changing what words come out of your mouth? The chapters in this book are about making changes in our lives.

This book is about becoming more like Christ.

We typically do not like change. Yet, anything that is not changing is not growing. If something is not changing, it is stagnant, or it is dying. Don't be a part of the living dead. The living dead are people who are living simply to exist. There is more to life than just existing! That is why the TGIF (Thank God It Is Friday) mentality has always bothered me. I don't want to live just for the weekend. I want to live each day to the fullest. To live each day to the fullest means that I become more and more like Christ. I try to see things the way Christ sees them. I deal with life situations the way Christ dealt with them. I think about life the way Christ would think about life. That is what it means to become a new creation in Christ. It is a life-long process. It is a challenge for every day. It involves change by the power of the Holy Spirit. Let God change you. I promise, you will like the new you. Become a new creation in Christ!

Epilogue

When I tell people that I have been writing a book, they ask me, "What is it about?" After I tell them, the response has been the same, "When it is published, I want to read it!" That is encouraging! I hope that when people read this book, they will recommend it to others. I hope that I will be able to share the contents of this book with other people by speaking in conferences or at churches. I am giving this book as an offering to God. God can use it however He wants. I simply want to be available to Him in any way He wants to use me. I am still a work in progress. I am still on the journey of becoming a new creation in Christ. I hope you are too!

Postscript

Years ago, when I counseled married couples, I wanted them to have a clear picture of what a healthy marriage looks like. I read many books and articles but was unable to find a clear description of what a healthy marriage looks like. So, I came up with my own description of a healthy marriage. That description has five components. My wife and I have done a marriage retreat where we spent an hour sharing our experiences about each of these five components of a healthy marriage. I have often shared them with couples in marriage counseling and asked the couple to rate their marriage in each of the five areas. Some couples have said that they need improvement in each of the five areas. That admission on their part gave a basis of where changes needed to be made. I have started writing a book about what a healthy marriage looks like using these five areas. We will see what God will do in the lives of people through that book!

About the Author

Russell Frahm is a retired minister living in Merritt Island, Florida. He has been married to his wife, Karen, for over forty years, and they have four children and seven grandchildren. He enjoys writing, speaking to groups, traveling, boating, and playing sports. When writing, Dr. Frahm likes to write about having good, healthy relationships and growing in the Christian faith. What he finds the most challenging about writing a book is to make the material practical and life-changing for the reader. When Dr. Frahm gets older, he hopes to help people have the best life possible. His advice for other writers, young and old, is to connect your heart to what you write.

Photographs

Our camper

The Frahm Family

Building a fence with Steve

Football uniform

Inflatable kayak

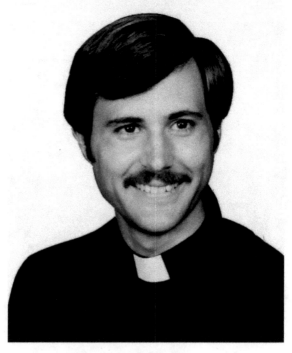

Seminary graduation

CPSIA information can be obtained
at www.ICGtesting.com
Printed in the USA
BVHW051828270623
666442BV00014BA/625